THE
PASSION
FACTOR

Silvia Leal and Jorge Urrea
Foreword by Kecheng Liu

THE
PASSION
FACTOR

LONDON   NEW YORK   SAN FRANCISCO   SHANGHAI
MEXICO CITY   MONTERREY   BUENOS AIRES
MADRID   BARCELONA   BOGOTA

LID Publishing Ltd
One Adam Street
London
WC2N 6LE
United Kingdom

31 West 34th Street, Suite 8004,
New York, NY 1001, US

info@lidpublishing.com
www.lidpublishing.com

A member of:

Printed in the United Kingdom

EAN-ISBN13: 9781910649039
Translation: Don Topley
Cover design: Juan Ramón Bautista
Typesetting: produccioneditorial.com

First edition: December 2016

For our children, our greatest teachers.

Contents

Foreword

Most of the greatest progress in human history has been driven by innovation. The use of fire and tools witnessed the beginning of human civilisation; the use of steam power brought us into the industrial age; the technology of electric power transmission and transformation gave our economic and cultural evolution another boost; the birth of information technology marked the dawn of the information era and is still revitalizing our day to day life.

As has been pointed out by many, the speed of innovation is exponentially increasing. As innovation can substantially improve what already exists, its importance has long since been recognised. The ability to innovate is regarded as one of the most important qualities for individuals, organisations and even for nations. In this world with increasing abundance of material and information, and the astonishing speed of socioeconomic development and globalisation, business success is largely determined by the ability to innovate. Innovation helps businesses to distinguish themselves from others by exploring new business models, providing new services, and redefining customer relationships. Consequently, to understand the nature, value and process of innovation is of great importance.

Innovation is self-reinforcing as it allows the emergence of new technologies, products and services, new ways of working, and even new culture. Newly developed components will in turn accelerate the innovation process. While the conversion between innovation and technology is not automatic, optimising the interplay between innovation that leads to new technologies and the new technologies that accelerate innovation can be seen as key to realising the value of innovation. However, in general people encounter difficulties in mastering the transformation process between innovation and technology.

In fact the interdependencies between innovation and technology are so sophisticated that it is not enough to just embrace innovation from the perspective of the outcomes such as technologies, products, services or other artefacts which we call the concrete sphere. An innovation is unusually not incidental, but arises from knowledge, experience and expertise that have been accumulated from previous practices. What has accumulated can be only accessed through the use of notes, language, data, information and other forms of signs which constitute the virtual sphere. The effective interplay between the concrete sphere and virtual sphere is essential in conceiving innovation and benefiting from it.

The concrete sphere is characterised by objects, technologies, artefacts, processes and people and their actions; while the virtual sphere contains notes, languages, data and information that can be regarded as a digital or sign-based sphere. The benefits brought from an innovation often lead to an increase in productivity which takes place not only in the concrete sphere but also in the virtual sphere, in the form of human knowledge, skills and capabilities. In turn, the virtual capital (i.e. knowledge, skills and capabilities) accumulated in the virtual sphere may potentially lead to innovation. How do we understand, measure and benefit from the relationships between the two spheres?

Organisational semiotics, the doctrine of signs applicable to business and organised activities, offers a rich philosophical and theoretical foundation for understanding the connections and interactions between the concrete and virtual sphere. Organisational semiotics treats a business as a system consisting of human activities involving both concrete and virtual resources. For a business organisation to attain its objectives, activities must be organised and coordinated through norms. The norms govern the behaviour of the members in the organisation towards the goals. The norms are a set of specific guidance for human behaviour which is acceptable within a certain context or situation. Norms have two functions, namely the descriptive and prescriptive functions. The descriptive function, which is also called informative, guides humans to understand the facts and phenomenon of the concrete sphere; meanwhile, the understanding or the knowledge is reflected in the enrichment of the virtual sphere. The second function of a norm is the prescriptive function, which is also called normative. As such, a norm instructs the members in performing actions or governs human behaviour. Customs and patterns of behaviour will become norms over time which reflect some regularities and help others to predict and coordinate if necessary.

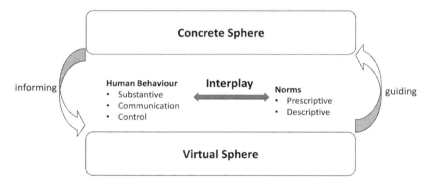

Innovation through interplay between human behaviour and norms.

Following an organisational morphology, human behaviour in the concrete and virtual spheres can be categorised as substantive, communication and control behaviour. Substantive behaviour directly contributes to the objective and realises the intended value of the innovation; and such behaviour may lead to changes in the concrete and virtual spheres, including transferring the philosophy from the virtual to concrete sphere and interpreting the facts from the concrete to the virtual sphere. The second category, communication behaviour, is about informing the relevant stakeholders in the innovation; such behaviour aims to coordinate those who are involved in the innovation to take the right actions with the right resources at the right time and space. An example of such behaviour is the scheduling of human and other resources based on the intended work content and procedure, i.e. to inform the relevant people about when and what actions are to be taken, and by whom. The third category, control behaviour, aims to reinforce the overall connection between the concrete and virtual sphere, particularly to monitor and evaluate substantive and communication behaviours. An innovation that creates value for a business will normally require a team to work together effectively in all three categories of activities in both the concrete and virtual spheres. Leadership in a business organisation that sets up an effective organisational morphology and promotes the culture of innovation is critical in building an innovative organisation.

This book addresses innovation in an organisation from an extremely interesting perspective by looking at the organisational culture. Unlike most other literature, it treats the organisational culture as an important asset and offers practices for managing and benefiting from the culture's pivotal role in innovation as compared to other factors such as economy and finance. Innovation may bring economic and financial value, but only focusing on these factors may be counterproductive. The authors logically argue that leaders in an organisation must find out how to hone their business acumen at the same time as they unleash their passion for innovation. Furthermore, the book provides an effective methodology and a set of tool for entrepreneurs, managers and business leaders to nurture innovative behaviour in three different dimensions: people, the business organisation and motivation. The authors recognise the impact of an individual's innovation potential in terms of three key factors: creativity, technological profile and psychological profile. In relation to the individual's impact on innovation, the importance of women is explicitly discussed with convincing propositions and suggestions on how to benefit from female talent in organisations.

The authors propose their Innova 3DX methodology to categorise different influencing factors into three dimensions which are the creative ecosystem, individual innovative potential and the passion factor for innovation. The dimension of the creative ecosystem includes the factors within an organisation or a workplace that contribute to innovation. Such factors include corporate culture, work climate, leadership and management style. The second dimension zooms into the individual innovation potential and the influence of individual factors on organisational innovation, e.g. creativity, relationship with new technology, and psychological profile which are the restraints on innovation capability. The third dimension focuses on the passion for innovation, which motivates both individuals and organisations to engage in innovative activities while taking advantage of the creative ecosystem and individual creative power. By understanding the factors that lead to innovation, organizations will be better positioned to lead, promote and sustain it.

Professor Kecheng Liu
Director of Strategic Initiatives
Henley Business School

Introduction

The rules governing the market are changing at dizzying speed. To succeed, or even just to survive, original and risky ways to compete must be sought. Ideas about how this might be achieved sometimes arrive out of the blue, a process we like to call serendipity. You can sometimes be lucky and come up with a random discovery that'll produce a market success, but this is rare. If you want ideas to develop, you have to be ready.

Businesses and professionals who aspire to innovation leadership have to understand that innovation is not the direct outcome of finance, but the result of human creative energy. Investing resources in R&D is essential, but it is not enough by itself. You must be prepared to extract the maximum return from this move, which means that anybody who wants to stand out from the background and grow in spite of the turbulence must learn how to efficiently manage their intellectual capital and creative energy. In other words, they must find out how to hone their business acumen at the same time as they unleash their passion for innovation.

The Passion Factor provides the formula for doing just that. It explains how to apply the Innova 3DX methodology which stops creativity from leaking away and catalyses creative energy so that the "innovation engine" is on full throttle. Supported by facts and data, it reflects on the importance of extracting the maximum potential from both genders, as learning how to capitalize their difference is essential to become a leader in the field of innovation.

This book has two parts; the first one, from the first to the twelfth chapter, deals with the efficient management of innovative behaviour; and the second part, the last two chapters, covers the profitability of women in the workplace.

Chapter 1 explains the part played by innovation in the building of a new global economic order shot through with uncertainty and new challenges, yet also opportunities that must not be ignored. It shows that innovation has become established as an essential tool for facing current challenges as well as those still ahead in the future. As you would expect, it reveals the way that innovation has become a vital instrument for companies battling to regain the road to growth.

Chapter 2 introduces the Innova 3DX method, which sees innovation as an essentially human process that must be managed via three routes: the creative ecosystem, innovative potential and passion, the biological engine that drives us to act. From another angle, we see how we are conditioned by our environment, our skills, our creative blocks and our motivation for innovation.

Chapters 3, 4 and 5 focus on the nature and the operating mechanisms of the first dimension, the creative ecosystem, plus the three factors that shape it: corporate culture (as regards innovation and technology), the work climate and leadership and management style.

Corporate culture includes the values, standards and thought patterns that define and shape behaviour in a company, which means that it is one of the factors that best identifies its essential nature. A culture that *genuinely* values and encourages change is essential if the whole of the company's individual creative potential, and hence organizational potential, is to be released. Equally vital is a culture which understands that the new technologies are more than just a passing fad – in other words, innovative (sub) cultures and technological (sub) cultures will need special attention.

The work climate is the factor that includes the measurable elements of the environment which in turn, influence commitment and motivation in the workplace.

This covers the physical space, ethical and moral framework, emotional and spiritual aspects. Businesses that lack any of these factors will be afflicted by an ailing culture that will oppose innovative behaviour and inhibit the efforts of all those who possess talent and the skills to use it.

Leadership and management style is the factor that defines how the strings of the organization are pulled. The most innovative companies will be those with innovative leaders. This calls for any leadership style that is based on orders and supervision be set aside in favour of an example-based approach demanded by this new era. What are needed are professionals who lead by example and have the ability to intelligently catalyse the creative energy of their teams so that they produce profitable ideas. This change will not be easy for leaders who are used to spending their time ensuring that things are done the way they would do them themselves. Now, it will be a question of survival for everybody.

Chapters 6 to 9 focus on individual innovative potential, and this is monitored in terms of three factors: creativity, technological profile and psychological profile (self-esteem, optimism, locus of control and learning orientation). This way, a holistic view of creative capacity is incorporated, since we now step beyond the traditional focus (creativity-centred) to take in the internal forces that lead to the release of our total energy – or, of course, stifle it.

The primary factor (chapter 6) in this dimension is creativity, a concept very similar to innovation. Given that an innovation is the result of an idea with application and market entry, the line that divides them is very vague: potential profitability. It is this which has led to a large number of businesses launching actions aimed at encouraging individual, and hence corporate, creativity. And these have often achieved good results, but with a wider perspective, they could have aspired to much greater things.

Factor number two (chapter 7) concerns your relationship with new technologies. Since they are without question the main engine of innovation within a company, efforts must be made to ensure that every single staff member is prepared to build them into their everyday activities and, of course, that they are able to use them to channel their creativity.

The third factor (chapters 8 and 9) is the psychological profile, a concept which includes those features of the personality that are able to paralyse your creative power – or give free rein to innovative energy to the extent that it reaches its own limits. Being aware of this and correctly managing it (including self-management), empowers individuals, as well as groups, getting the best from everybody but also creating synergies from their team actions. In the world of open innovation, where all drive and all are driven, it can be no other way.

Chapters 10 and 11 cover the third dimension of the method: the passion for innovation. This represents the biological engine which, given a creative ecosystem and a certain level of innovative potential, will drive us to act, to attempt to innovate and to create. Its power is determined by your motivation and the braking effect that derives from your fear of failure. What this means in real terms is that you are driven by hopes that your efforts will pay off and the emotional value you place on the results you hope to achieve. And you're similarly held back by the fear of something not turning out well.

Many companies are already aware of the importance of these factors, and are therefore investing a great deal of money and effort with the aim of promoting innovation. In most cases these organizations concentrate their efforts on concrete dimensions or factors, such as creativity and corporate culture. They are definitely looking in the right direction, but to achieve 100 per cent calls for a wider perspective. This is why Chapter 12 explains how the procedure can by monitored using an overall viewpoint. It includes a step-by-step guide that shows how to develop a diagnostic of the brakes and catalysts involved in the procedure; a tool which will allow you to proceed safely and securely along the road to innovation leadership.

The chapters devoted to the factors that comprise the method follow the same content and layout plan. Initially, Silvia Leal sets out an academic, research- focused view – the outcome of her doctoral studies. Specifically, she offers a theoretical outline of the nature of each factor and includes a number of examples to explain their essence and how they work. She goes on to describe how they affect innovative behaviour and she includes a simplified version of her self-assessment tests which reveal the situation's status and the need for possible corrective actions.

The second part of the chapter covering these factors is the work of Jorge Urrea, who adds his insight management, a term that refers to the self- management that arises from an in-depth and clear perception of the environment and of oneself.

The style of this section is somewhat profound, brought to life by stories about the writer's ancestors, painters, dictators, governors, entrepreneurs, managers, customers and non-customers, and illuminates different, authentic action approaches that teach us powerful lessons for life and work. He includes introspective disquisitions on innovation, self-esteem, fear of success or failure, managing your own life, motivation, culture, optimism etc. All of this is examined from a wide range of cultural viewpoints and disciplines (Taoism, Zen, gestalt, phenomenology, philosophy, history and/or economics).

The second part of the book focuses on the financial risk of under-use of female talent. Chapter 13 explains how to capitalize the female workforce, together with quantifying the financial impact on organizations. The Insight management section consolidates this approach and acknowledges women's value from a social dimension but above all, due to profitability.

Chapter 14 covers the importance of women in new technologies. In this chapter, false assumptions leading to the phenomenon of female depopulation will be exposed together with the solutions for a problem that, believe it or not, has an easy remedy.

And of course the book is coloured by the gender perspective, because men and women are not the same, and it is essential to learn to manage these differences effectively.

The Passion Factor is the outcome of a long, detailed research project in which thousands of companies and professionals took part. The interesting but unexpected conclusions, which were commented on by international publications such as *Forbes,* are of interest to all.

The key to emerging strengthened from all kinds of crises is in the book in your hands right now. We make one suggestion for those choosing this pathway: passion and insight. The rest is just a matter of time.

01
Innovation Radars

1. The Geo-Innovation Radar

The figures are devastating. The US owes more than 50 per cent of the growth experienced by its companies during the latest decades to innovation generated by new technologies. These are the data supplied by the AAAS (American Association for the Advancement of Science), and they send a very clear message: new technologies are no passing fad. Quite the contrary: they have played an essential part in positioning the country as the leading world power of our times.

The figures for the US are not an isolated case. Thanks to new technologies, European Union countries achieved a GDP (Gross Domestic Product) growth of 25 per cent and a productivity increase of 55.6 per cent between 1995 and the beginning of the latest crisis. This reflects the fact that a significant proportion of its management understood the value of these tools and has been able to build them into its processes of innovation, transforming them into powerful and effective growth levers.

And yet at the present moment we can see how, although these economies are struggling to regain and consolidate the road to growth, it seems no note was taken regarding how they managed to get where they were: digital innovation. The ranking of innovative countries according to the Global Innovation

Index (GII), worked out by Cornell University, INSEAD and the World Intellectual Property Organization (WIPO), clearly reflect this.

If we take a look at the 2015 ranking we see that the USA (world economic leader) is listed at number four, closely followed by rivals such as Singapore, in a field currently led by Switzerland. On the other hand, seven of the European Union economies are found in the Top 10. This group consists of Sweden, the United Kingdom, the Netherlands, Finland, Denmark, Ireland and Germany. But not all the EU nations are doing so well from this point of view. We can include here countries such as France and Spain, which, despite their leading positions in the last International Monetary Fund's world economies ranking (positions 6 and 12), are seriously lagging in the classification which measures their efforts as innovators, where they hold positions 18 and 28 , a long way from where they should be striving to be.

In other words, innovation has become established as a key factor in economic growth. And yet the countries that now occupy chief positions are failing to maintain their leadership as innovative powers. This is the case for countries such as the US, France and Spain. Are we witnessing the beginning of a new world economic order taking place backed by this kind of ranking? Might it be that these countries will lose their current leadership positions if they fail to change their strategy and implement emergency measures to stimulate innovation? The facts and experience suggest that not only had they better do so, but that they had better do so now.

Now let's change the focus and try to picture the scene from a global perspective. What's happening in Latin America? Are any efforts being made to apply the statistics and lessons learnt from the US and the European Union?

A further look at the IMF world rankings shows that Brazil holds ninth place. And yet we are surprised to see that its position as an innovator is a long way back, at number 69. Why? Has this country with its huge growth potential opted for a deliberate strategy to adopt a different course? Or is it, perhaps, that something is not right?

We could assume that innovation is not so important in Brazil. This is one of the largest countries in the world, with an area covering 47 per cent of South America and with a population of around 200 million. This has led a number of analysts, such as Goldman Sachs, to see Brazil as one of the five countries set to dominate the economic world in the coming decades. This group includes Russia, India, China and South Africa, known in the world of international economics by the acronym of BRICS.

So perhaps the business fabric of Brazil has no need of innovation, given that it has the possibility of using other opportunities or tools as growth and development levers. But let's take a look at the situation from another angle: what if innovation – or the lack of innovation, were their Achilles heel?

Chile leads Latin America in innovation. This economy, at position 42 in the IMF world ranking, occupies the 44th position in this global classification. One of the reasons behind this is that the government is fully aware of its importance as a source of growth, jobs and entrepreneurship. This country has very successfully undertaken a number of actions that have had the effect of stimulating interest in and enthusiasm for innovation within its ecosystem of businesses and entrepreneurs. Worthy of special notice is its Innovacion.cl project (www. innovacion.cl), a digital medium designed to boost creative and entrepreneurial behaviour. Thanks to attractive content that deals with technology, innovation and entrepreneurship, this medium has become an effective transformative force, one that people are quite excited about.

Chile has also begun to teach by example. Moving from theory to practice, it has launched a range of high-impact concrete measures intended to raise awareness and promote these new concepts. One example is that the government approved a draft bill that would allow for the creation of a company within 24 hours at a greatly reduced cost, thanks to the electronic signature. As with many progressive measures, its establishment has not been to everybody's taste, given that there are group interests that do not gain by the decision. We trust that it will not remain frozen at the draft bill stage.

And this is not unique. In the same vein, this country has launched a new R&D law which provides significant private investment tax incentives for research and development projects. These are just a couple of examples of a proactive policy aimed at overcoming the old models' resistance.

What happens next? What will the economic repercussions of these concepts be? According to IMF forecasts (2016), Latin America will grow by 1,5 per cent in 2017 despite challenges, fatigue and market tensions. And even so, the forecast for Chile stands at 2,1 for this same period. My bet is that their innovation-boosting policies and strategies have had something to do with it.

The situation in Colombia and Peru is very different. In the IMF classification they hold positions 41 and 51 respectively, but in the innovation rankings, they fall to positions 63 and 71. Why are they not tempted by Chile's approach? These countries are already moving forward with genuinely promising initiatives, such as iNNpulsa Colombia (www.innpulsacolombia.com) and Innóvate Perú (www.innovateperu.pe). There is no doubt that they will be opening up valuable opportunities.

We now want to focus more closely on Asia, particularly China, and also Israel. If we fail to mention them, given the pages devoted to them by the media when innovation (or the lack thereof) is the subject, this analysis would be incomplete. So we start with China, the number two economic power on the world map.

Although to a great many of us China is not seen as an innovator (an imitator, rather), its GDP percentage of investment in R&D has climbed by around 20 per cent a year since 1999 and forecasts suggest that within another decade it will have stolen the US' leadership in this field. Even so, right now it holds position 25 in the ranking of innovative nations. So what is its problem? It's the difficulty of transforming investment into innovation.

China shows that innovation is not the direct outcome of budget allocations in this area. You need an ecosystem which is kind to innovation and suitable management. To achieve this, efforts must be made to build such a bridge, and this requires an understanding of the status quo and expectations regarding the results to render such investment profitable. This is no easy task, given the existence of tough political hurdles – obstacles that require a great deal of thought and effort to overcome on a road that looks far from smooth.

Israel also devotes a high percentage of its GDP to R&D, some 4.7 per cent to be precise, which establishes it as the world's leading nation in this respect. But the results are very varied. Tel Aviv (the economic centre) shows this clearly. According to a study carried out by consultant Startup Genome and Telefónica Digital, Tel Aviv has become the major entrepreneurial system in the world after Silicon Valley. It has managed to oust cities like New York, London and Paris which had assumed that such a leadership position was naturally theirs. Its recipe contains four ingredients: a highly developed financial ecosystem, a strong entrepreneurial culture, effective support mechanisms and a healthy supply of talent.

Not to put too fine a point on it, this country not only invests considerable resources in R&D, it has also moved forward and established a sound foundation for ensuring that its investments are profitable. This has meant that despite the fact that it only ranks 35th as an economic power, Israel occupies position 21 in the innovative countries ranking and has established itself as the number three economy with the most companies on the NASDAQ, after the US and China. In the same vein, it has managed to persuade companies such as Google, Hewlett-Packard, Facebook, Intel, Samsung, Microsoft and Apple to set up their R&D facilities on its soil, so that the list now includes over 250 organizations. Without a doubt, this points to a more than promising economic future for its entrepreneurs.

To round off the geo-innovative radar, we should spare a line or two for the case of New Zealand, as this is a country that provides a shining example that's opposite the case of China. New Zealand occupies position 53 in the world economies ranking, way behind the leaders. But in the innovative countries classification, it stands at a much sought-after number 21, despite the fact that it invests less than 1.5 per cent of GDP in R&D. This figure seems very low compared with, for example, the European average, which is higher than 2 per cent. How can that be? What lesson do the New Zealanders have to teach us? It turns out that in fact their case does have an important lesson for us. It is certainly important to devote resources to R&D, but that alone is not enough. It is necessary to learn to efficiently manage the innovation process to ensure that the return on this budget allocation is as profitable as can be.

If we analyse what it is that has led New Zealand to occupy this position in the land of innovation, we realize that it has not simply been luck, but rather, the result of a successful, detailed plan of action. Known as Growth Through Innovation, the strategy launched by its government in 2002 has borne fruit. New Zealand has generated a powerfully innovative ecosystem with the capacity to get the best from each agent (business, university, entrepreneur, etc.) both individually and also via their interactions. This country has worked out how to generate an effective system of collaboration where a joint vision is shared by all: united for innovation.

Since our aim is to offer an overall perspective that will help explain the value of innovation – not produce an exhaustive study of the factor by geographical zone or country – we can leave the analysis here. Nevertheless, given that the exercise is extremely interesting and sources of data can be easily accessed, I would like to encourage readers to find out more about those countries that have not been included. This will certainly help to reveal fresh answers to the questions about innovation. You may explore the same sources of data I have used, or investigate others, such as the European Union's Innovation Union Scoreboard (2016). The conclusions will be the same: innovation is a vital resource, a key to economic development and essential to entrepreneurship.

2. The Innovation Leadership Radar

Every year the European Commission publishes its *EU R&D Scoreboard,* a report which reflects the efforts devoted to R&D by those countries most concerned with this factor. This information is supported by the addition of its market development, which makes it possible to obtain a broader perspective on each of them and assess the impact (or absence thereof) of the investment made in each case.

It also performs an analysis of the 2,500 companies who invest most at the global level, representing, in total, the equivalent of 90 per cent of the market's total investment. According to the latest listing, companies investing most in R&D and holding the Top 10 positions are Volkswagen, Samsung, Microsoft, Intel, Novartis, Google, Roche, Johnson & Johnson, Toyota and Pfizer.

The US placed five of its companies at the top (Microsoft, Intel, Google, Johnson & Johnson and Pfizer), the remaining five come from Germany (which actually occupies first position, thanks to Volkswagen), Switzerland (Novartis and Roche), Japan (Toyota) and South Korea (Samsung). By sector, we note that pharmaceuticals and biotechnology occupy four positions while the rest are automobiles & parts, electronic and electrical equipment, software, technology and computer services.

Curiously, all the companies that form part of the Top 10 have made significant increases in this field in the past year.

Figure 1.1 Top 10 R&D Investors, According to the European Commission

world rank	Name	Country	Industrial sector (ICB-3D)	R&D 1 year growth	Sales 1 year growth
1	Volkswagen	Germany	Automobiles & Parts	11,7	2,8
2	Samsung	South Korea	Electronic & Electrical Equipment	10,0	-9,8
3	Microsoft	US	Software & Computer Services	5,8	7,8
4	Intel	US	Technology Hardware & Equipment	8,7	6,0
5	Novartis	Switzerland	Pharmaceuticals & Biotechnology	0,8	2,9
6	Google	US	Software & Computer Services	24,3	18,9
7	Roche	Switzerland	Pharmaceuticals & Biotechnology	2,4	1,5
8	Johnson& Johnson	US	Pharmaceuticals & Biotechnology	3,8	4,2
9	Toyota	Japan	Automobiles & Parts	10,3	6,0
10	PFIZER	US	Pharmaceuticals & Biotechnology	26,9	-3,8

The European Commission offers an interesting view of the companies that have done a lot to improve their products, but are they the most innovative companies? Perhaps all we can really say is that these are the companies that invest most in this area. This doesn't deprive them of value, but it does highlight the fact that we should take a step back in our analysis if we want to be able to answer the question: "Who are they?"

The investment of resources does not always produce results. I suggest that we look a little further than measuring the effort made (input), and also look to classifying the results (output). This is what Thomson Reuters has done with his awards: Top 100 Global Innovators[1]. In this case, what we are looking at is not exactly a classification, but a list that includes all the best positioned companies in this area; a methodology that highlights the relevance of the patents obtained regarding which success, volume, global reach and influence are factored in.

Would these, then, be the most innovative companies? That could be the case, although this information only allows us to pick out those that have obtained the greatest value because of their patents.

Innovation means more than just patents or new products. The definition that the Organization for Economic Cooperation and Development (OECD) includes in the Oslo Manual (2005) makes it very clear: "the introduction of a new, or significantly improved, product (good or service), a process, a new marketing method or a new organizational method in the in-house practices of the company, the organization of the workplace or external relations". This is the clearest and most widely accepted definition internationally. For this reason, although the two previous classifications offer interesting and valuable perspectives, they fail to provide any answers to the question about which companies are the most innovative. Where, then, can we find the answer?

Each year, recognized classifications worked out from an alternative point of view are published. One very interesting perspective is that of Fast Company2016[2]. They produce a ranking that incorporates very diverse sectors and companies of all ages. In their latest ranking, leadership went to BuzzFeed, for having transferred its specific brand of virality to deep political coverage, personal and critical essays, and breaking and in-depth global news. Even so, the focus of their analysis is very concentrated on the US.

One other classification system is that of *Forbes*[3], developed to a large extent in keeping with the principles that guide the Oslo Manual. In this case, leadership tends to go to very powerful companies with more international images.

But again, we are forced to ask whether these companies are really the most innovative.

The most innovative companies may be the huge multinationals, but they could equally be small family firms. They could be private companies, but public bodies could also fill the bill, old-established organizations might fit, as could start-ups. The most innovative companies are those that are capable of harvesting the totality of their intellectual and creative potential and that can channel it efficiently towards the generation of profitable ideas.

This book is dedicated to them, to all those companies and professional entrepreneurs who are staking everything on being a part of this new, as yet unpublished, ranking, but that will set the future for the markets. A promising future awaits them all: innovation leadership.

02
The Innova 3DX Method

1. The Genesis of the Methodology

This isn't a new subject of discussion, arising from the tough situation now facing many governments, companies and entrepreneurs. Neither is it a well-worn political discourse, emerging from the grinding economic crisis still ravaging a number of countries. And yet with every passing day, the nub of the matter is obvious: without innovation there is no salvation.

The rules of the game are the same as they ever were. Innovation is no new strategic option devised to fight the battles of the marketplace. If we perform a perspective-drawing exercise, we see that apart from the way that problems (and their solutions) are formulated, essentially little has changed. Innovations always lie at the heart of the responses produced in the eternal debate about the elements that determine the success of an organization.

Some readers may suspect that I take my inspiration from Tom Peters (1985), deemed by *Fortune* magazine as the "Ur-guru" (the guru's guru), in the wake of publications such as *A Passion for Excellence*, where he established that the golden rules for business success could be boiled down to two: marketing and innovation. Naturally I agree with him, but in order to track down my sources of inspiration we shall have to travel slightly further back in time.

Peters' thought coincides to a large extent with the philosophy we already examined some decades back in the work of Schumpeter (1939) in his *Business Cycles*, which in turn drew on the earlier contributions of David Ricardo (1817) in *On the Principles of Political Economy and Taxation* and Adam Smith (1776) in *The Wealth of Nations*.

That is why, even though a great deal of water has passed under the bridge since their day, it should be mentioned that these writers – who realized even then the importance of technological advances and innovation for economic growth and entrepreneurial success – were pioneers.

And yet, despite the wealth of literature and research on the subject, innovation continues to be surrounded by questions with no clear answers: why must we innovate? It uses up resources, it requires time, there are opportunity costs. What happens if I decide not to join in with this old-fashioned approach? Why is it such a crucial element for both the new gurus and the old economists? Is it, perhaps, a matter of faith? Where are the figures? How does it affect my business and me? Where are my own figures?

And there are still more questions. If I decide on this route, what happens if I don't know how to start? Why are there so many books published on the subject, and yet they all seem to say the same thing? There they are, always the same answers – creativity and the culture of innovation. Are these two factors really the formula for success?

This is how the innovation phenomenon makes its appearance, and along with it comes what we might call "innovation sophism" (Σοφία, the Greek word for wisdom); a new stream of thought in which now a very popular target for writers who want to position themselves as gurus. They promise to reveal the secrets of this almost magical process that allows businesses to ignore the scorn of the markets. Unfortunately, in many cases, they are accompanied by even more questions, and with them, fresh secrets yet to be deciphered.

This is why this work is different. All the answers have been checked in detail, and the work provides an effective methodology for use by anybody who decides to go for innovation: the Innova 3DX Method, a genuine tool for the most experienced operators – as much as by the beginner.

The Innova 3DX Method supplies the keys whereby the innovation machine can operate "at full throttle", so those companies and professionals who decide to invent and reinvent themselves will be able to find the transformative energy from their own motivation. It is designed so that anybody will be able to build the conditions that guarantee not just survival, but a healthy dose of success.

Answers are not only given to the recurring questions surrounding this phenomenon, but also to new ones, such as: what are the keys that encourage innovative behaviour? Do gender differences exist in this field? How can you unleash passion for innovation?

To achieve these goals I conducted extensive and in-depth research in which thousands of professionals took part. The interesting but unexpected conclusions, already reproduced in international publications such as Forbes, will leave nobody unmoved.

2. The Three-Dimensional Management Model

Innovation is not the direct result of finance; it is the fruit of human beings' creative energy. Metaphorically speaking, innovation is the result of the combustion of three elements:

people, organization and motivation. If these three factors are efficiently managed, the result is powerful creative energy (new products, business, markets, etc.), but if they are managed badly, the result is simply incineration.

Businesses that have decided to stand out from the statistics and grow despite marketplace turbulence will have to implement mechanisms which minimise creativity leaks and establish, as a matter of course, the incorporation of all intellectual and creative capital into a new ideas generation machine. These businesses must ensure that they are developing their organizational skills to the maximum. For all those businesses and/or professionals keen to lead in this field, the Innova 3DX Method will be a very useful tool.

This strategy looks upon innovation as an essentially human process that must be managed via three dimensions: the creative ecosystem, innovative potential and passion, the biological motor that drives you to act. In other words, you could describe this as the management of the environment, your capacity and creative blockages, and your motivation for innovation.

It can be used by businesses and by their managers and directors, and also by professionals or entrepreneurs who want to integrate innovation into their lifestyles.

2.1. First Dimension: the Creative Ecosystem

An environment that raises barriers against innovative behaviour will stifle the efforts of everybody who has talent and the skills to innovate. In such organizations the creative spark will be extinguished. This means that businesses must prepare to identify and eradicate the brakes that restrict those who confront the process, and, naturally, to set the mechanisms necessary to speed up the process.

In other words, companies that are keen to lead in this coveted territory must work to build creative ecosystems capable of unleashing innovative power. To do this, three factors must be monitored: the corporate culture (as it applies to innovation and technology), the work climate or environment and the leadership and management style.

The corporate culture – standards, values and thought patterns – has an obvious influence on behaviour. If it's positive, it can lead us, motivate us and even excite us. On the other hand, if the culture is confused or disorientated, if its values and standards are unclear or damaged, it becomes a weighty burden. In other words, a culture that genuinely values and encourages change is essential if individual and organizational creativity is to be unleashed. It will also be essential for everyone to understand the value that all of the new technologies have assumed, so they can be built into corporate strategy.

The impact is very easy to see. How many of us would take the risk of implementing an innovation if it were considered ill-advised, or if it clashed with the corporate culture? And what if we were breaching the standards?

Naturally, there will always be exceptions. If your boss supported you in these endeavours maybe you'd take the risk, but would you do it over time? My guess is that you wouldn't and that you'd soon see a good manager looking for another job. Of course, the manager might stay on and turn into a leader behind great change, which would be wonderful but I still believe that in most cases, that manager would end up taking a walk.

The work climate is a particularly complex concept, covering everything from the objectivity of the physical space to the subjectivity of the ethical, moral, emotional and spiritual framework. The mechanism whereby its influence works is very simple: companies that fail to provide a positive work atmosphere cannot hope that their employees will make any efforts to come up with creative ideas.

It's worth just thinking about this for a moment. How many of you would take bother to make some valuable suggestion to your firm if you felt cold all the time in the office, or if the chair was uncomfortable or the noise made by your colleagues continually interrupted your concentration. Yes, you might come up with some valuable suggestions, but they would likely be about eliminating those problems.

Let's take it a step further and include the non-physical aspects. How many of you would take the chance to innovate if you felt you weren't respected, if you lived each day in actual fear, or if you felt you'd get no recognition for any suggestions made? Personally, I have no doubt that I wouldn't take such a chance.

So here is factor number three, the management's managerial and leadership style, the ways they pull the strings that direct the organization. Its influence is obvious: if a company fails to provide its employees with the resources needed to innovate, if a boss never communicates with their employees, if you have no autonomy and if improvement is never rewarded, how could a company hope to stand out as innovative?

Many companies are already aware of the importance of this dimension – and its component factors – and because of that, invest a great deal of effort and money to establish suitable creative conditions. In the majority of cases, these organizations focus their efforts on the work climate: are they providing suitable physical conditions? Are they providing a good ethical, moral, emotional and spiritual framework? They also question and address the corporate culture: does the company appreciate innovation? Is it part of the company strategy? These questions are essential if innovation is to flow, and for many, they are a good place to start. But how many companies check to see whether their managers are harvesting all the creative potential that their teams actually have to offer?

Strange to say, in most cases this is one of the factors with the greatest influence on innovative behaviour. Yet it is the one to which the least attention is paid. It could be because this kind of self-assessment can hurt. On the one hand, some people are hurt simply because they feel they are being interrogated. Does somebody think they aren't doing their job well? And on the other hand, those who have good reason to fear being interrogated will also feel hurt. Such a process may reveal that there are indeed factors that should be changed and maybe there are others that could be done better.

It is important to highlight the fact that in order to manage these three factors efficiently, it is essential to understand their mechanism of influence on an individual basis. No less important is that the relationship maintained between these elements must be grasped. Your innovative behaviour is conditioned by your work climate and its corporate culture. But the final effect of these two factors on each one of us is largely shaped by managers' leadership and management styles.

Imagine that you work in a highly innovative company that provides a very positive work environment – but, alas, the boss is, unfortunately, "anti-innovation" (there are still some to be found). Can any innovative efforts be made? How likely is it to happen? Innovative impulses will soon be frustrated. If it's possible to rely on support from outside your area, you might make the effort, but even so, your impulses are likely to be destroyed, at least in part. If it doesn't happen because of fear it might be because that "anti-innovation" boss stamps on it personally. In any case, something isn't working, and that means an opportunity is being lost.

Figure 2.1 First Dimension: the Creative Ecosystem

The Innova 3DX Method includes a model for the management of the creative ecosystem which includes the work climate and the corporate culture as two *"sine qua non* factors", elements where careful alignment with innovation is essential to ensure that the creative engine is operating at full throttle.

Management such as this is rendered complete by the inclusion of a system to monitor the leadership and management style, a factor that must also be aligned with innovation. The difference is that now you're looking at an element that conditions the final impact of the two prior factors, which might turn into an obstacle to its influence on your innovative behaviour (and hence an obstacle to its influence on actions to stimulate it), or to the contrary, into an effective lever to intensify it. All those organizations that now have their actions focused on the work climate and innovation culture will find their next step on the road to optimising organizational creativity in this driving factor.

2.2. Second Dimension: Innovative Potential

Innovative potential is much more complex than creativity. One's relationship with new technologies (do I like using them? do I like innovating with them?), self-esteem (me? am I sure I can do this?), optimism (is this going to turn out well – or will this too go down the drain?), the locus of control (does it depend on me? just me?) and learning-oriented direction (a new challenge? a new opportunity?) strongly influence creative behaviour and must be correctly understood and managed. If they are not, then a large part of all that innovative potential will simply evaporate.

This means that new management models that appreciate human capital from this new perspective must be adopted. Unfortunately this is no easy task, because managing people from this angle calls for skills and competencies that many traditional managers – often focusing only on efficiency – never learnt to develop.

Those with the nerve to attempt it will have to monitor their innovative potential in light of three factors: creativity, technological profile and psychological profile.

Innovation arises in the human spirit and you find yourselves forced to be creative. A clear consensus exists on this and that is why many actions designed to encourage innovation are focused on creativity. But are they effective? They definitely produce valuable results, but in most cases, the results could have reached far greater heights.

For creative energy to be unleashed, it is essential that one's personality doesn't stand in the way. Some aspects of personality, such as self-esteem and optimism, may be potent accelerators, but they may also operate as brakes, preventing one's total potential from being expressed. Will you give free rein to creativity if you feel pessimistic, or if you feel that everything will turn out badly? And what if your self-esteem is down around your ankles? You won't take those kinds of chances; you'll be paralysed by your own blocks.

On the other hand, the role that has been taken up by new technologies now means that all members of an organization must be ready to integrate them into their day-to-day activities.

Figure 2.2 Second Dimension: Innovative Potential

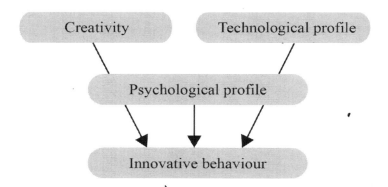

Therefore, the Innova 3DX Method includes a management model of innovative potential that includes monitoring our creative and technological profiles as "*sine qua non* factors". These elements require suitable management to harvest each individual's personal genius, and hence optimise the organizational profile.

This kind of management is rendered complete by monitoring the traits of the personality, a factor that conditions the final influence of the prior elements. This could turn into an obstacle, or on the other hand, become an effective lever. All those organizations that now focus their actions on creativity will find the next step to developing their competitive intelligence by defining their own limits in this "driving factor".

2.3. Third Dimension: the Passion for Innovation

Passion could be defined as a powerful appetite or love of something. It is a force that can get the best out of each of us, and can channel it towards our goals, needs and desires. Its manifestation is accompanied by optimism, enthusiasm and energy, which is why its effect on the journey towards success is more than merely important.

In actual fact, according to acknowledged experts on modern management such as Gary Hamel (2007), passion determines nearly 35 per cent of the probability of success of an action. This is really something that, in a world in which 85 per cent of the population goes to work in body but not soul (Tower Perrin, 2003), companies who want to stand out must not forget. And of course, those intending to lead in innovation must keep it in mind constantly.

In the field of innovation, it is passion that reflects this biological force or engine which, given a creative ecosystem and some innovative potential, will encourage us to act and strive to innovate and create. The power of its drive will be determined by our motivation for innovation and by the brake applied by our fears of failure.

In more real terms, the motivation to complete a given action arises from the emotion caused by the probability of succeeding and the emotional value attached to the result. And yet that force urging you forward into action will be checked by fear of failure, be it great or small; it is always present because it is part of being human.

You can define fear of failure as the dispiriting thought that something will turn out badly and bring negative consequences along with it. This fear is accompanied by thoughts that have very serious effects on your behaviour, that then condition your efforts and professional achievements.

Some people will wonder why we haven't included fear of failure as a personality trait. The answer is simply that its impact is so important that it must be included as an independent factor so that it can receive the attention it requires.

Figure 2.3 Third Dimension: a Passion for Innovation

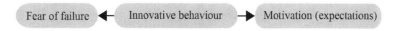

Fear of failure ← Innovative behaviour → Motivation (expectations)

Thus, the Innova 3DX Method includes a model for managing passion that incorporates monitoring our motivation for innovation and for fear of failure. These are the key elements.

For companies seeking leadership in the field of innovation, this dimension will be of special interest, because once satisfactory creative conditions have been established and the measures required to encourage maximum individual creativity have been set up, this will be the key to achieving everything else.

3. So Now What? The Innovation X-Ray

How can you efficiently manage these three dimensions? How can you measure them? How can you prescribe the actions necessary to ensure that they act as catalysts?

The first step will be to understand the nature of each of the factors incorporated into the methodology. Next, the Innova 3DX Method proposes that you take the pulse of each of the different forces involved in the process. This task will produce, as its end result, the "innovation x-ray". This tool provides a valuable diagnosis of the elements that "move" so that creative energy is invoked and implemented, and also of those elements that place a check on them. It will also be very effective for identifying corrective, preventive and/or predictive measures in this field.

In just a few words, the task begins with a listening exercise that reveals the status of each of them, which in turn provides the basis for the actions required for stimulating innovation so it can achieve its maximum potential. Everybody wishing to do so will find here the guide they need for developing their own three-dimensional (3D) x-ray.

03
The Creative Ecosystem. First Factor: the Corporate Culture

1. Culture and Subcultures

A good corporate culture can help you compete in the marketplace and becomes the basis for generating new competitive advantages. Conversely, a confused or disoriented culture, where values and standards are unclear or damaged will become your greatest burden.

The concept of the "corporate culture" finds its origin in Peters' and Waterman's bestseller, *In Search of Excellence,* 1984. The authors take the term to mean the standards, values and thought patterns that define and shape the behaviour of a company. This is not something found in a manual, nor does it form part of some book of instructions, but there is no doubt that it exists and it is a fact that it has a powerful effect on the way things are done in a business. Indeed, it is the single factor that best identifies the nature of an organization.

A corporate culture is all but set in stone. However, its constituent parts may evolve and even change completely over time. This change is slow and often goes unnoticed, but it can drag the corporate culture away from the strategically decided-upon pathway. If this happens, corrective measures will need to be deployed in order to survive.

How can you exercise any influence over this uncharted territory? What are the standards, values and thought patterns you must focus on to convert a stuck culture into a catalyst for creativity? In other words, what elements within a corporate culture degrade entrepreneurial genius, and which ones boost it? The answer is simple: the (sub)culture of innovation, and the (sub)culture of technology.

1.1. A Culture of Innovation

An innovative company is one that can transform scientific and technological advances into profitable products, services or processes; it realizes that uncertainty comes loaded with new challenges but also with fresh opportunities that cannot be ignored. These companies know that a culture which genuinely values and encourages change is essential, since this will endow the process with sustainability while adding power to it.

The organization that decides to develop such a culture may find itself facing a dangerous natural barrier: resistance to change. The human mind recoils from anything that is out of the ordinary. Resistance to change is inherent in human nature. This means that companies will have to ensure that the firm culture of innovation they wish to build and consolidate can persist in facilitating the creative processes of the individual.

So how is this done? Where do you begin? What must you focus on? And how can you measure where you've reached – your progress? The answer is in the 4 Ms technique, which covers four basic development areas that require attention for developing and maintaining a true culture of innovation: Movement, Mission, Medium term and Motivation. Fix this little picture in your mind, and you won't forget:

Figure 3.1 The 4 Ms of Corporate Culture

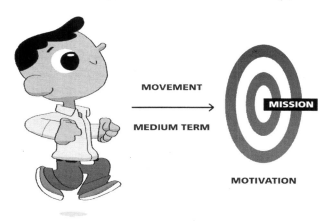

Companies keen to lead in the world of innovation for the long term must maintain a proactive attitude to change. They must learn to transform and be transformed reactively and proactively. This process may be powered by small innovations, but these may also be very disruptive. What matters is to become part of the change, like a transformation engine, so to speak. In other words, these organizations will have to build a culture that encourages movement (M) both before and after, taking small steps as well as big ones.

Movement itself does not always achieve anything. If movement is backward, the finish line is always getting farther away. If movement is in circles, you just get dizzy and probably end up falling over. You may not always move in a straight line, and again, small steps may be taken in reverse. Even so, all these movements may be valuable, may be a part of the journey, but what matters is that you have a course: what direction do you *want* to move in? To decide that, you need a mission (the second M), and perception, to throw light on the why and the wherefore of the company. This will generate a sense of corporate solidarity and explain the existence of the organization, and also illuminate the part played by each individual in the overall machine. This will make it much easier for all members of an organization to work together towards common goals and to inject their creativity. Things will make sense.

The third M provides the time frame. Increasing numbers of businesses are recognising the value of innovation and are deciding to adopt this new 'fashion' to get out of their rut. Many launch actions designed to encourage creativity and/or an innovative culture and seek to unleash their creative potential in the short term. There's nothing wrong with that as far as it goes ... but it's usually the way it's done that fails.

Not many innovations develop like this. The generation of profitable ideas is a process that takes its own time and cannot be hurried. This means that a short-term mentality is genuinely dangerous here. Right thinking demands a change in business attitude which in many cases will be a complete about-face. Or, to put it another way, you have to change the chip. Long-termism? Naturally you shouldn't lose sight of the long term; it is certainly there, but for now, focusing on the medium term (M number three) is probably enough.

The final M is motivation, the emotional engine that generates the energy you need to achieve your goals. To work to fulfil a mission you need to be motivated, or at the very least, you mustn't be demotivated. You have to feel a real connection with the company and feel that it matters to you. This calls for developing an environment that motivates the staff to give 100 per cent; to be involved, body and soul.

Given that not everybody is motivated by the same things, nor to the same extent, each company will have to work out its own formula. How? One good way is to begin by example. Innovative companies are managed by leaders who are innovative people themselves. In the long term it has to be this way. This means that when a non-innovative leader decides to take this path, the first thing he or she will have to change will be within him- or herself.

The second suggestion is to inject a little adrenalin into the company's bloodstream. Adrenalin is a hormone secreted by our suprarenal glands. It acts very quickly to mobilise all our available energy to tackle a situation involving tension or fear. When it flows through your veins, your muscles become tense, your pupils dilate and your heartbeat increases. You're preparing for fight or flight. But it also charges you with vitality and makes you alert, strong, directed and focused. In other words, it can be very beneficial.

How does this affect the workplace? Adrenalin is present in our relationship with the company. It plays a very important part, acting in a positive way by contributing to your motivation, or in a negative way, by demotivating you. This means that the injection of a little positive adrenalin may be very effective. This isn't difficult and doesn't require complex mathematical formulae or wide-ranging statistical analyses. If you just listen carefully to your teams, they'll tell you what it is that motivates them.

The third and final suggestion lies in a sense of humour. This is the basic key to maintaining a positive state of mind. It is the necessary ingredient for a satisfactory personal and professional life. Organizations keen to construct an innovative cycle that will last in the long term would do well not to forget it.

1.2. A Culture of Technology

Our lives are surrounded by a spiral of change that has revolutionised our socioeconomic environment. Digital technologies are built into our everyday activities at every level. They have built their own space (cyberspace) where it is possible to construct a new identity and an environment that is also governed by its own culture (cyberculture). The digital world has also revolutionised the nature of our social relationships, the way we communicate, and has even created a new lifestyle. New concepts have developed in its shadows, such as distance learning, cyber commuting, e-business, e-banking, e-administration and even remote medicine. And this is far from a complete list – these are just examples of new realities that are becoming more firmly rooted by the day.

This historical acceleration has also transformed the rules of the marketing game. Under this new paradigm, information technologies have taken up positions in opposition to traditional productive factors, finally positioning themselves as the main pillars of the business world. These tools have explosively disrupted their operating mechanisms, something that many see as a new industrial revolution. This has led the communications media, politicians and many public bodies (among others) to call on us all not to miss out on this tide. And yet, in reality, do you have to form a part of this revolution? Why do you have to take on these new technologies as part of your corporate culture? Can't you leave things the way they are? Actually, no. You have to catch the tide. The consensus is unanimous and rests on two powerful arguments:

The first is based on the importance of incorporating it into in-house procedures, which leads to improved quantity and quality of information available. This has a direct impact on productivity and flexibility, creating greater response speeds and capacities with regard to market needs. This argument considers its effect on the overall value chain, since it allows for instant communication, at low (or no) cost, to stimulate and accelerate the globalisation of business.

The second argument focuses on its role as a generator of new business channels and models. These technologies have transformed traditional businesses, not just by establishing a connection with the end customer, but by making interaction possible. The outcome has been the destruction of a great number of businesses that failed to understand the need to adapt or that were unable to adapt correctly, and also includes the streamlining of businesses that were unthinkable without new technologies. They are a fundamental part of the birth of the most powerful businesses to be found now in the markets.

The benefits, however, are much greater than this. These technologies have grown into an essential tool for achieving both current and future goals. Challenges such as energy efficiency, pollution and the future of transport systems can only be tackled with this tool in hand. And, of course, they are key in sustainable socioeconomic development, particularly for those countries that are bearing the brunt of the crisis.

In other words this is not merely a straightforward development – it is an explosive change that cannot be undone. The new digital world has made it possible to achieve unprecedented productivity levels, bringing along with it a generation of new business models which had previously not been technically feasible. In this paradigm, new technologies play a central part.

This said, it must not be assumed that the mere adoption of new technologies alone is sufficient. Organizations that aspire to leadership positions as innovators will have to adapt their standards, values and thought patterns to these changes which are here to stay. These businesses must be sure to include these tools as part of their core competencies and overall strategy, supply correct training, encourage the use of these tools and provide the resources necessary to enable all who have the necessary courage to innovate as they can. This is the only way that they can drive the reactive and proactive transformation demanded by the markets.

How can this be achieved? How do you grasp opportunities and challenges that result from new technologies? Example-based leadership is a good place to start. Putting recognition and reward actions into play for the benefit of those who take up the challenges would inspire more of the same. But each organization will have to work out its own formula based on its own identity and situation. The secret is to understand that technology is part of the movement forward, and must be adopted with a proactive attitude aimed at shaping new markets.

2. Innova 3DX for the Corporate Culture

A culture that genuinely values and encourages change is essential if the totality of the business genius available is to be liberated. Equally essential is a culture that understands the importance new technologies have assumed and that can import them as part of the company's essence. Is it possible, however, to assess their importance in more than mere words, to evaluate their relevance for any company at all, including mine and yours?

The corporate culture is normally taken to be solely responsible for between 10 – 15 per cent of innovative behaviours. Some may believe that this is a low figure, but would you still feel that way if they raised your pay by 10 per cent? The same applies here, so explaining between 10 – 15 per cent of people's behaviour is, indeed, explaining a great deal.

In this factor a significant gender difference is noticeable. More specifically, it tends to affect male behaviour to a greater extent than it does female behaviour, something to be watched if full available potential is to be harvested from both groups.

Nevertheless, its role in the innovative process does not end here. The corporate culture exercises a clear influence on our potential and passion for innovation. We should focus on this, with motivational expectations used as an example (a factor from the model's third dimension).

Suppose that you work in a company that does not innovate, that traditionally rejects change. And let's also suppose that it is proud of that. Hard to believe, I know, but it is still true of some organizations. What do you think about the likelihood of an innovative idea gaining traction? Would you invest your energy to do battle in support of it? Maybe you'd take your idea elsewhere.

The outcome is that, whatever the direct consequence, there will also be an indirect consequence, one that plays a very important part in the overall context. This means that it is essential that entrepreneurial acumen be very carefully monitored if is to be developed to its maximum.

Figure 3.2 Corporate Culture Test

Instructions: score your opinion on each statement from 0 – 10, 0 being the lowest and 10 the highest. Use decimals if you need them.

The Innovation Culture		
1.	I work in an innovative company.	_ _ , _
2.	I work for a dynamic company.	_ _ , _
3.	Change is encouraged in this company.	_ _ , _
4.	The company really appreciates those of us who strive to innovate.	_ _ , _
5.	I believe that innovation plays an important part in company strategy.	_ _ , _
Average score		_ _ , _
Technology Culture		
1.	The new technologies are part of our day-to-day work experience.	_ _ , _
2.	The company makes use of new technologies to be competitive.	_ _ , _
3.	The company makes the most of the internet's potential.	_ _ , _
4.	The company makes the most of mobile phone apps.	_ _ , _
5.	The company makes the most of the potential of social networks.	_ _ , _
Average score		_ _ , _

Result: from 0–3.5 (inclusive) very low, from 3.5–5 (inclusive) low, from 5–6.5 (inclusive) satisfactory, from 6.5–10 (inclusive) very high.

Figure 3.3 The Corporate Culture Quadrant

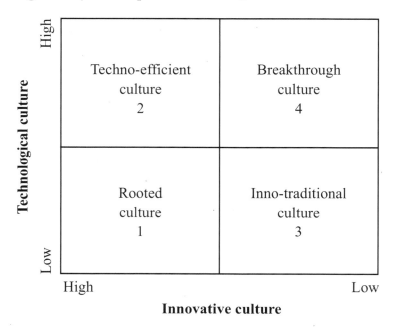

Square one contains companies that have a culture which does not favour innovation, where the use of technology is also not encouraged. These are companies rooted in their past, companies with a "rooted culture" that could well threaten their survival in the environment of very volatile markets.

The next square contains organizations that are keen use technology, but which fail to innovate in comparison with their competitors. These are companies that adapt to the demands of the market in the style known as *second adopters*. These businesses have a "techno-efficient culture", but lose out on the profitability available to those espousing digital leadership.

54

Square three comprises those organizations which are innovative in the old-fashioned sense of the word, where technology is not the engine of creativity. These are businesses that will not occupy leadership positions in a digital world, but which will take advantage of vacant niche markets that can provide adequate profit. These are known as having an "inno-traditional culture".

Square four comprises the organizations that have a "breakthrough culture"; companies which value innovation and new technologies that provide them with a good foundation for being competitive. If they manage matters intelligently and with imagination, they have a promising future.

Companies which bank on establishing a breakthrough culture should remember that if such a culture is to be consolidated, it must be built up steadily on the basis of example given by management and by each individual.. Naturally, projects can be set up which will facilitate the process, but if the foundation is not laid, it will not be consolidated over time.

3. Insight Management and Corporate Culture

It is said that culture is what is left when you've forgotten everything. So, using the proverbial glass as a metaphor, what is left at the bottom of the glass when water evaporates are values, usages and customs.

Culture in general and a culture of innovation and technology in particular, has an enormous effect on identity, whether company routines are performed well or badly. But it is ethereal, hard to nail down and even volatile when we remember that in the information society, the speed of change is much greater, making culture as fragile as fine porcelain.

Many years have elapsed since the collapse of Lehman Brothers and the subsequent public and private banking and economic crashes; and yet the creation of a maximum risk speculative culture – of an 'everything goes' attitude and the looting of present and future resources has not yet yielded to a new backdrop that will hide or at least tone down the grotesque reality that lies behind it.

We should be recovering and boosting the spirit of those entrepreneurs who are totally committed to an idea, a project or a product, and who invest their passion, their lives and their joy in bringing it to fruition as though it were one of their children. What matters is that it should work. Every individual will leave his or her footprint, personality, values and customs behind in this process, as will those who come after, taking up the reins of business in their turn.

From so many different footprints just as many different cultures and companies will arise, so first ask yourselves: what is it that shapes a culture nowadays? Is it the result of management, the founding father who framed the image, or what? In a real case, you'd have to be careful how you treat such a source. If the present management team is a figurehead or a point of reference for all, you're in no position to gradually change it, as this would lead only to confusion. If a charismatic founder is the focus, he or she must continue to exude a presence that is more impressive than anyone else's if paradoxes and contradictions are to be avoided. Sometimes nothing is what it seems.

In my work I have listened to people complain bitterly of ghastly experiences in frightful environments where respect for the rights of their workers was sadly lacking. It was not so much that values, standards and thinking patterns were just bad – they bordered on the obscene. You might think that such companies would have to be multinational armament manufacturers, bent on destroying the Amazon rainforest or some such, but this was not the case. The fact was that some of these companies, institutions and other bodies, possessed genuinely distinguished façades, were recognized for their high level principles, beliefs, and attitudes that not only did they not defend, they actually betrayed them to the extreme.

I recall the evidence given by a manager of a well-known theme park, a genuine delight to young and old. He had been given a fright because the performers who moved here and there through the park wearing disguises decided to take off some of their outfits and drift about half-costumed to show that the low wages they were paid left them not just underfed but positively starving. It is impossible to sell magic and fantasy while paying your workers a pittance. Sooner or later it will explode in your face.

This was not an isolated case. Other examples come from all kinds of institutions, public and private, cultural and social, intellectual and leisure-focused, some of them at least theoretically very remote from maximum profit goals. I know some NGOs where the staff was in danger of awarding themselves the supposed virtue of being in the right because they were defending the moral high ground. Alas, many of them turned out to be little better than humanitarian terrorists, forever lobbying for "their" truth which was frequently a long way short of actual reality. Confidentiality agreements prohibit me from mentioning names, but anyone who reads newspapers will find numerous examples of institutions and people who discarded the initial spirit of the organization.

From the worker's point of view, anybody with a modicum of intelligence and the freedom to do so will vote with their feet, that is, they will simply decide that, "If it's no good here, I'm going elsewhere". I remember the case of one member of a foundation's management team who received a note asking him to look for a secretary for the CEO. The candidate needed to be "someone who had no sense of dignity", because the humiliation that person would have to tolerate from the boss, which unfortunately would be repeated down the company ladder, would be intolerable otherwise. Evidently anybody with dignity, vision and capability would be swift to leave before they, too, became corrupted. Anyone who could adapt to these kinds of values and practices would end up, whether they liked it or not, turning into yet another thug perpetuating the "culture" of the place.

I might add here that it isn't a good idea to have enemies anywhere, because sooner or later the past will re-emerge. But if you must have enemies, choose them very carefully because you will end up modelling yourself on them in how you act, the weapons you use and the attitudes you adopt, etc.

But let's return to paradoxes. How is it that companies that in theory have nothing to do with the moral high ground, operating for example in the fields of technology, pharmaceuticals, insurance or finance, manage to have cultures that are so superior to the rest? What's different? How is it that people always want to work for them?

The secret is always the same: people. If a person is centred and suggests an idea with a clear, positive and enthusiastic attitude, that person can evoke the same trust and sense of involvement in others, and over time this will spread throughout the company. By contrast, if you start with a management system based on fear, exploitation, envy, unfair competition, etc., you won't make much progress. "The apple never falls far from the tree," as the old saying goes.

If the company invests in training and its employees' well-being, people will want to stay there with those who care about them and give them room to "create" and continue growing and developing their abilities.

Jobseekers should always bear in mind that it isn't just a good job they need, but a place where they also feel at ease, where the culture suits them. Should they find that they possess higher standards than their employer, they will find themselves demoralised. By way of contrast, a person without scruples and a burning desire to get on at any price could turn out to be a blight on a defenceless company that will then begin to fester from within. We must all be vigilant.

Since we've looked at corporate culture from the point of view of a person joining a company, let's do the same from the company's position. A crucial question is: what is the right moment to replace a manager who is threatening the culture's continuity? The answer is always the same: it depends. Some companies strive to maintain a culture that will persevere, that is rigid and immutable and which if lost, would take their essence with it, while others feel that if they don't evolve they will become extinct. In technology, it is necessary to have the ability to change with the times, and quickly.

In the management/company relationship, there exist companies with a very strong culture of change, where management is very quick to adapt to the position/culture. There are other companies that have a greater mutual commitment to having the staff and business grow together, where time allows for a two-way interaction process.

These are the companies of particular interest to us in this study, since these are the businesses where innovation is best observed, where it is rewarded and capitalised on, and where the two-way bond strengthens connections, motivation and hence productivity.

The temptation to continually look for fresh individuals, who will perform better than their predecessors, professionally or personally, reflects the assumption that the grass is always greener on the other side. This does not mean that change can always be avoided, but it is a fact that someone who is already on the inside, with training and motivation, may produce great results.

Special mention should be made of female integration and the effect this has on innovation. The myth that the truly creative master is always male has been promulgated by a patriarchal society where women are deprived of resources, room and even time. So you shouldn't be surprised that the majority of the examples of great creativity come from men. But progress has been made in education, principles, training and economic independence where women are concerned. Women and their creativity have become a very valuable resource which no one can afford to ignore.

We can only look forward to the time when, instead of seeing a man or a woman, we see a person, and that person's creative and productive capacity. Little by little, in more and more organizations, there are racial changes too. Some of us may already have arrived and know that diversity will always provide gifts for those who know how to make the most of them. The alternative is to continue with our ancient resentments and prejudices which demonise change and halt evolution.

With regard to the culture of innovation, analysed according to the four aspects, let's recapitulate the way the action moves forward in one direction, with a time frame and a mission.

Which direction is the right one? That is something you will know once you start moving and you analyse the journey, because no journey exists that can be traversed in a straight line. In life, success is always a consequence of many movements, some good, others not so good, but where something is learnt with each movement. Lesson one, then, is that fortune favours the brave. Move – and take the risk of making mistakes.

So, let's return to the matter of which direction to take. How many directions are there? According to Taoism there are five great directions. Not just four: north, south, east, west and centre. Although this may seem contradictory to what has been said above, awareness may urge you to move to the centre, without actually moving, and anchor yourself, not because you are frozen, but because it is the best move. Don't underestimate it. If you take a look at the swing from one side to another taken by various governments in political economy, you will realize that many would have done better to develop what was already in position and encourage it to mature, rather than dart off in another direction to do something fresh – to innovate, indeed. Do by all means innovate, but please, let it be for the better.

In any case, if you intend to fire an arrow, first centre yourself, look carefully, check the wind, imagine the journey the arrow will make through the air, feel how it will penetrate the target, and then draw and fire. According to the Zen master archers, beginners should never have two arrows. The thought that if you miss with the first you can always succeed with the second means that your concentration is never complete. If you are not convinced about your business, then don't bother to launch it, don't waste your energy and your time firing your arrow. Wait for kinder weather. If you are not convinced then you will never devote yourself to anything or anyone, neither a partner nor work contract, but if you have already done so, then live it as though there was never any other possibility. "There are no arrows left," should be your mantra. This is the only way that you will do your work correctly.

In this sense and contrary to what many think, seeking added time merely anchors you in the past and makes it harder for you to be absorbed into the present and the new adventure you've decided to embark upon. I recall an engineer who hired me because he wanted to get out of a loop of wasting hours every day wondering whether he should go back to his old company some months after he had left it. On the personal front, we all know someone who can't stop sending love letters to the ex-partner in the hope that love lives on, and can be relied upon if the new partner fails to deliver. Let go of the mooring rope, explore other seas, because you can't reach home from the harbour of the past.

Let's move on. The fact is that while everyone's aware of the importance of culture, motivation and mission are just as important. For a lot of companies these qualities are very hard to communicate, especially in times of fast change where survival under threat means that values and traditions shift so quickly. What happens at the macro level happens at the micro level, where as far as the individual is concerned, the mission is a mystery.

Here are the keys to look at: time, the moment, and the tempo. Think for a moment about a surfer who decides that he will catch his wave when *he* decides, and not when the wave arrives – crazy, right? But that's what so many people try to do, professionally and personally.

Many people fail to understand that life and work have their own rhythms which are built in, and they resist them like King Canute tried to on the beach. Others feel the solution is to plunge *into* the waves and devote all their strength and adrenalin to making some progress against them. They get the feeling that they are moving somewhere, but it's an illusion.

All too often the Canutes just become furious, or attempt to escape from the situation by slumping into passive-aggressive depression and being beaten down. "The system doesn't understand me; what the boss wants is impossible; the kids are leaving me no time to live." These are the people who say that if you want work done well, then you must let them do it "in my own way, in my own time". The others will go down the path of thyroid malfunction, the thyroid being the organ which, among other things, regulates the consumption of energy necessary for the activity involved.

A large number of professionals suffer from hyper- or hypothyroidism. When I say a great many, I should add that there is a significant gender difference in this area. Many women handle their jobs (although some men too) in a cool and effective way, the same way they do at home, and when the 'to do' list is nearly all crossed off, they become anxious, fearful to exist unless they are constantly on the go, executing the next task. This is a real problem. If they want to build sustainable personal and professional careers, they need to review their lives and work out how to deal with what is in the present.

With greater or lesser speed, and varying degrees of madness, we all mount this same sort of train at some point in our lives, and get off again at another point, without actually being seen as crazy for our whole lives. But if you want to leave this sort of madness, you have to be aware of it: you have to listen to yourself and to what's happening around you, learn to see the waves as they really are, and accept that the world is not going to operate at a different rhythm because somebody else says so.

If tempos are as important as rhythms, moments are just as important as time periods: some people make their way through their working lives complaining that too much is demanded of them in the short term, that they can't deal with the sudden spikes, and that they just can't win.

But don't be misled, I'm not saying that all businesses have the same kinds of spikes. You'll have to work that out for yourself, maybe with the help of a professional. Some jobs have really violent spikes which are then offset by really relaxed periods for recovering; the life of a top level athlete would be an example. Some companies just burn out their staff and then hire more fresh staff to be burnt up.

Both company and worker must keep the medium term in mind as the time period for creation, innovation and the management of resources. Anybody who operates all the time at a rate that looks like the final sprint, as if there were no tomorrow, is dangerously compromising their health. Place your trust in working with stubborn discipline. It often turns out that creative processes make their appearance quite suddenly in the medium term, following an internal maturation process or an interesting construction and deconstruction process that can neither be hurried nor postponed, and that usually arises unexpectedly. In other words, pressure is OK, as long as it's justified and the term is neither excessively long nor short; the medium term is the right one. Stress, no. Activation, yes.

In any case, you have to take hold of your life's steering wheel and be responsible for it: if you decide to invest your life in a project, a company, a marriage, a family or whatever it is, you absolutely must learn to keep your finger on the pulse and dance only to that rhythm, with your head held high. If you don't, you will constantly be broken, swamped, and anxious; the horizon will seem invisible, and your demonstrations of strength will only damage your professional and personal output. You won't be happy, nor will you be able to change the external rhythm. Believe me.

If you want to surf your way through life, remember the famous sentence which my brilliant English teacher Mike used to repeat every week during the long years when I was a trainee diplomat, a time when I was frankly drowning, but which now I understand and hand on to you:

Keep your head above water!

04
The Creative Ecosystem. Second Factor: the Work Climate

1. Aspects of the Work Climate

Work climate is a concept usually found in management literature. The basic definition is attributed to Litwin and Stringer (1968). According to them, it concerns the measurable elements of work environment that have an effect on commitment, motivation and behaviour.

So what are these elements, and how do they affect us? How can we measure them? How do they influence your innovative behaviour, and are there gender differences? What can you do if you find that your own climate is unsatisfactory?

There are a large number of factors that make up the work climate of an organization, and in order to understand them and manage them, it is very useful to divide them into four aspects: the physical space, the emotional aspects, the ethical and moral framework, and the spiritual approach.

Figure 4.1 The Aspects of the Work Climate

The influence of the physical space is clear and has led to ergonomics (the discipline that studies the phenomenon) which has become an abundant source of literature. A basic requirement of a good environment is adequate space, good lighting and suitable climate control. Obviously ventilation, cleanliness and hygiene conditions need to be monitored and managed. It is also important that efforts be made to reduce or preferably eliminate distracting factors such as noise. This is obvious to everybody, but it still has to be monitored. In fact, it is probably worth taking a closer look at noise as an example.

Workers who are continually exposed to high frequencies (in the region of 4,000 Hz) will lose auditory sensitivity in this area of the hearing spectrum through damage that over time expands into the region that includes the human voice. The frequency of this pathology, known as occupational deafness or hypoacusis, is so great that each year it occupies one of the top spots in the lists of occupational diseases. It is generated as the result of a progressive degeneration of the ciliated cells in

Corti's organ (in the inner ear). It often starts without the victim being aware of it, and is made worse by virtue of the fact that it is degenerative and there is no treatment for it. In addition, it frequently develops along with the constriction of the blood vessels, an increase in heart and breathing rates, and a reduction in the activity of the digestive and cerebral organs.

You might think that this is an extreme case, not the sort of thing that office workers need to concern themselves with, yet nothing could be further from the truth. How often do you fail to notice the deafening sound of the building's air conditioners until they are turned off? How many of you have worked in noisy environments packed with endless chatter and the sound of telephones – which you've adapted to such that you don't even hear them? The effect of these situations can lead to tiredness, headaches and loss of sleep. Hypoacusis is just one example from a long list of occupational pathologies published by the International Labour Organization (ILO). Many, in fact most, are the result of economic problems, aggravated by the arrival of new technologies. They now include new afflictions such as "mouse curse" (carpal tunnel syndrome), a lesion caused by the compression and inflammation of the wrist nerve as a result of extreme postures during prolonged periods of intense and repetitive work.

In other words, a good physical environment must be in place not just to pass conventional work and safety audits, but to ensure that staff are able to contribute their full potential. The opposite case could prove very expensive.

Even so, good health as far as the workplace is concerned means more than just physical matters. The World Health Organization (WHO) states the following in its articles: "Health is a state of complete physical, mental and social well-being, and not merely the absence of infections or diseases"[1]. This means that the work climate must also include positive emotional, ethical and spiritual factors.

Goleman (1996) stated that "it is impossible to separate skills from the social framework which supports them". In his opinion technical capabilities and managerial skills are essential to the competitiveness of a business, but they are not a differentiating factor. He insisted that what mattered was for organizations to be able to manage emotional well-being. However, he also pointed out that this was not an easy factor to monitor, since people respond emotionally in different ways to identical stimuli.

The ethical and moral framework is also an essential part of the work climate. It exercises a powerful influence on commitment and motivation. When people are uncomfortable in a moral framework, sooner or later they end up demotivated. Many suffer burn-out syndrome, a phenomenon recognized by the *Diagnostic and Statistical Manual of Mental Disorders,* (DSM, published by the American Psychiatric Association) as one of the problems associated with handling life's problems. Curiously, this also turns out to be an element that includes its own Darwinian natural selection process, since professionals with dubious moral constitutions do not remain in companies with strong ethics (and vice versa). In other words, the famous laws of attraction and repulsion apply.

Before moving on to the following aspect, it must be stressed that an important part of a company's ethics includes the fact that employees should receive fair pay. No business can expect its staff to give 100 per cent if they don't receive a fair reward in return. They might give 100 per cent in the short term, if no alternative is available, but it will not be sustainable. If a company's treatment of their staff is not ethical, sooner or later they will pay for it. As indeed they should.

I want to add a comment about spirituality, an element which, despite what many think, is not necessarily connected with religion. Robbins (2005) expressed this very clearly when he said that "organizations which promote a spiritual culture accept the fact that people have a mind and a spirit, that they seek a meaning and a purpose in their work, and that they wish to deal with other human beings, and be a part of a community". The author stated that spirituality has a positive effect on creativity, commitment and work satisfaction. In other words, people who think that the world of business and that of the spirit have nothing to do with each other are actually wrong, and this could turn out to be a very expensive mistake.

2. Innova 3DX for the Work Climate

The work climate alone is normally calculated as being responsible for between 5 – 10 per cent of innovative behaviour within both genders.

The way it works is very simple. If your office has poor lighting, if you aren't happy in your work, if you're surrounded by a questionable ethical framework, if you aren't respected ... will you try to be innovative? Why should you? Let someone else do it. .

Its effect on the innovation process does not end there. Just as in the case of corporate culture, the work climate exercises an obvious influence on our potential and passion for innovation. For example, do you feel optimistic if your office is plunged in lighting gloom, and your daily routine simply depresses you?

This means that a good work climate is an essential condition if the innovative machinery is to work at top yield level. Organizations that intend to optimise their managerial acumen must be sure to establish a good work environment, and manage it efficiently so that it continues to act as a catalyst.

Figure 4.2 Work Climate Test

Instructions: score your opinion from 0 – 10, with 0 as the lowest score and 10 as the highest. You may use decimals if you need.

Aspect 1. Physical space		
1.	The conditions or the physical space I work in are good.	— —, —
2.	Lighting is adequate.	— —, —
3.	The temperature is suitable.	— —, —
4.	The noise level is low.	— —, —
5.	I am able to concentrate.	— —, —
Average score		— —, —
Aspect 2. Emotions		
1.	I like my job.	— —, —
2.	I like the company I work for.	— —, —
3.	I'm happy in my work	— —, —
4.	I don't feel scared in my environment.	— —, —
5.	Fear does not exist in the environment.	— —, —
Average score		— —, —
Aspect 3. Ethics and morality		
1.	Management is prepared to acknowledge its mistakes.	— —, —
2.	Managers say what they think.	— —, —

3.	The company recognizes work well done.	__ __ , __
4.	The company rewards effort.	__ __ , __
5.	The company rewards success.	__ __ , __
Average score		__ __ , __
Aspect 4. Spirituality		
1.	I feel respected.	__ __ , __
2.	I understand the value of my work.	__ __ , __
3.	I understand that it is important for my work to be well done.	__ __ , __
4.	I am acknowledged for my work.	__ __ , __
5.	I feel part of the company.	__ __ , __
Average score		__ __ , __

Result: from 0 – 3.5 (inclusive) very low, from 3.5 – 5 (inclusive) low, from 5 – 6.5 (inclusive) adequate, from 6.5 – 10 (inclusive) very high.

Where, then, is the organization work climate? To answer, insert the averages obtained in the measurement test into the following table.

Figure 4.3 Work Climate Aspects Table

Space	Emotional	Ethical	Spiritual

Companies for which all aspects are satisfactory and in a stable state will have a "healthy climate". In these companies the work atmosphere supports innovation and allows it to develop.

But all those organizations that have problems with one or more of the aspects will face a serious challenge, because if they don't resolve the matter quickly, it could be the beginning of their end. It is not important which particular aspect is being demonised by these companies, because the fact is that the climate is unwell, and if this is not dealt with at the root, they may find themselves going out of business.

3. Insight Management and Work Climate

Talking about the work climate makes me think about the weatherperson and the way we fix our eyes on them and hold them responsible for all our happiness before, during and after the holidays. The same thing happens in the workplace: we often hold the company responsible for all the evil that occurs there, as though the company were something separate from all the people who work there and are a part of it, as if it were a diabolical being that swallows us and spits us out. Of course this is not true. Whether you work on the shop floor or as a manager, you want to generate a positive atmosphere and feel that you are in charge of your own life, and that you are working to achieve that. The company, via its bosses, can and should organize meetings to initiate and strengthen healthy and enjoyable connections, and identify and reject toxic individuals. It is the actual people who work there who will best know the state of the work climate and who should be most willing to help improve it.

In this sense, working with people from departments and companies that have survived mergers, I have met with both good and bad intentions: inertia-synergy and resistance-embargo. In the emerging climate we will find people from different business cultures enjoying different status and privileges and different operating methods and concepts, including different moral frameworks. Surviving the changes is a milestone. After a period of enormous stress because of fear of not surviving the changes, there comes a vacuum, where everybody tries to refocus their careers, relocate their mission, learn from the new environment and discern who the new allies are, the new bonds, what the new plans are, etc. Unfortunately, after months and even years many people will still be talking about 'us', former workers from such and such a company that failed to take on a new, wider identity, and they will muddy the atmosphere with caste differences. An insistence on perpetuating differences instead of progressing towards union is a perverse, selfish, individual or even group impulse which displays the death throes of the old company presence and its culture. Differences and belonging are opposite ends of the same spectrum, and if they are not used positively they give rise to ways of playing for or against, alone or in company. Their effect on output, happiness, focus and so on is obvious.

There are many types of business and many different kinds of climates or atmospheres. Aside from more conventional environments, there are trailblazers in garages or groups of colleagues gathered around ping-pong tables backgrounded by wildly painted walls, but all having a good time because they are producing and creating. These companies don't only guarantee that the air will be well ventilated and that the space is adequate, they actually create the environment. Lots of people think that these pioneers are geniuses, setting up their businesses in 24 hours, something that larger companies can't do. Are they wrong? Is a garage business better? Does it provide a better fit?

Frankly, I don't know. Each actual case has to be examined, but what is obvious is that increasingly there are more areas devoted to co-working and creation points that bring together innovation, contact and inspiration outside of the cavernous, goldfish bowl or closed door office.

So now you see efforts being welded to workspaces in the area of diversity. In addition to this, spaces where you can see and be seen as a professional are not only physical – evidenced by beautifully lit, multidisciplinary designed loft spaces – but also virtual: on the net, via portals, links, hyperlinks, blogs, social networks, etc. Work which brings together a variety of people, countries and sectors emerges from unparalleled wealth. However, in the following pages we will only contemplate companies where the space is not virtual, and employees are breathing the same air.

So let's look at the various types of environment and person: a company that fosters a creative environment with colours on the walls, meeting spaces and laid-back work areas, might actually find that it is immovably anchored by workers who are not comfortable in that environment, or who find themselves unable to make the most of it simply because they are intimidated by the new, by change, by their own rigidity and prejudice against what is different. And there are also very conservative companies that constantly stamp on any kind of spontaneity, brilliance, genuine movement or real creativity. This attitude will not only be their ruin, but also the death of the creative people who work there, who will end up being buried. If you think your life is miserable, change it, and stop complaining about the company.

As individuals and teams, we should first work out what kind of people we are, what we or our fellow workers need in order to be happy, to feel freer as regards creativity and its expression. You can't generalise, there are no universal prescriptions here, only those that you draft. There is a difference between having a workforce aged between 55 and 60, all old-style engineers with ties, briefcases and pockets full of pencils – and employing a majority of programmers or advertising people who are in their twenties, who wear flip-flops, T-shirts and untrimmed beards. It's no good just getting this group to wear suits, or the other group to enjoy coloured walls. Please – go with the flow, not against it.

Bear with the real situation in which your workers find themselves and take care of their well-being. Talk with them, listen to them, respect their creative processes in a supportive way and face the facts. Are they productive?? Set them free at the same time as you provide them with a framework of moral and spiritual security which they can cling to in tough times. In other words, be sure that they are very clear as to exactly how far they can go. This will bring tranquillity, because they need to know they can let rip within the limits while being aware of where those limits are. Limits guarantee a framework that works for the company and for the individual, so you're saved from going crazy in a world of unlimited creative expansion. Anybody who can neither be creative nor happy in this environment, or who fails to find their niche, will just have to keep on travelling until they do. The company must take care of the environment, talk to the individual and if that person cannot adapt, then he or she must be given the chance to look for another place to be happy in.

Of course, what I have just said must not be taken to mean we must seek sameness in order not to stand out from the crowd. Far from it. The quest for diversity is fascinating, as is the task of respecting and stimulating every person's individuality. Allow me to mention a few examples of diversity that are a little bit out of the ordinary: one of my clients is a rather well-known chef, but he's well over six feet tall. This means that on ergonomic grounds, he is unable to work in many of the country's kitchens, since they tend to be small, narrow and low. I know another man who was rejected from the army for being too short. Then there's a Muslim who would do better with an office where he can shut the door and pray at the appointed hours.

Variety is the spice of life. A business must welcome individuality and nurture it, and be enriched by a variety of people who bring along their talent as well as their variety. Given the global village we live in, companies should benefit from diversity, and make the most of it without making judgements.

Let's not forget that diversity starts with gender. What makes us different, makes us profitable. It isn't just the fact that it happens to be fashionable and more comfortable to have both men and women in the business. It's simply that being open to the presence of both sexes is the only guarantee that prejudice will not diminish what each person can offer. The natural tendency is to develop individually by balancing the masculine and feminine qualities that all carry within, and each at their own rhythm. A real team is balanced between male and female because it can better respond to bigger and more varied challenges. There are a few minor exceptions, but generally speaking, men and women keep things in balance, as a complete yin yang.

In the same vein, here is another genuine case, included as a rather non-obvious case of what people really need, rather than what they think they need. One female manager who seemed to be in need of absolutely nothing, and had merely dropped in for a chat, was actually locked into a situation where she felt enormously bored and anxious because she just didn't feel particularly useful where she worked. She had a boss who did everything himself, and she felt she wasn't allowed to contribute anything to help. She and her superior didn't communicate, and he never asked her to undertake anything complex, so she felt unjustified collecting her high salary. Her mistake was to value herself only in terms of results, of the image that was projected upon her, with the result that her self-esteem went through the floor and her sense of having a mission in life had vanished. Moreover, she suffered in silence, never communicating this situation, and thus never found an opportunity where anybody might justly recognize her achievements. It was a serious problem, made all the worse for going unnoticed. In fact had anybody realized, they would simply have advised her to carry on collecting her big salary and enjoying her lack of pressure. What she needed, in addition to clear communication with her supervisor, was to be entrusted with challenges that would make her feel necessary and important. So, you're not just the sum total of your successes and failures; you're much more, and also much less.

I think it's important for me to say something about psychological temperature, which can endanger a company's survival. A company's climate is not measured only by professional success, which for a professional team may be an important aspect of motivation; it can also be measured by caring relationships, personal bonds, a desire to be there, happiness – or, indeed, the opposite: unfriendliness, hostility or rejection. In some cases I've had clients that confess that a colleague of theirs is efficient, but their relationship doesn't gel, nothing seems to click, communication channels in general don't flow, and they don't create any kind of synergy between them. It's a waste, because in different environments both parties could be richer, more productive and positive.

Psychological temperature is not a common concept, or even an efficient one, since it depends a great deal on the culture of the country, of its people, their characters, and so on. So "Marriage, Italian Style" with Sofia Loren, requires much more passion and friction than a serene Romy Schneider style partnership. Each person and each coming together of two persons has to happen "in its own way", and each job and each environment at its own temperature. Everything that works is OK. Can you imagine a rugby team coming into a stadium for the Grand Final and warming up with Tai Chi? Can you picture a Japanese calligrapher or a Zen master gardener operating to the strains of ear-splitting heavy metal? To each their own, and with harmony.

Mention must be made of the fact that the work climate also depends on the presence of protection from other directions, such as the legal framework, trade unions, work inspectors, reconciliation tribunals, etc. All have varying roles of importance when it comes to understanding and favouring a given environment.

And let us not forget Corporate Social Responsibility (CSR) as a tool for generating a high-quality climate both internally and externally. There is no doubt that for many workers it is important to feel that they work in a company that not only complies with the law, but that also strives to make a positive difference. Improving the internal and external climate is a feedback loop that is always a positive, win-win situation that should never be underestimated, since it is profitable all the way around.

On the matter of the disturbing marriage between spirituality and business, let's go straight to its heart: if you're a manager, don't interfere, just relax and keep your nose out. Trust everybody to find the best way to stay centred, internally and externally connected and from top to toe, comfortable with their own positions, performing their duties professionally and existentially and feeling fulfilled and happy. All will be well. It isn't a question of urging staff to perform mid-morning prayers, meditation or Tai Chi (although it wouldn't do them any harm), because for some this would be very alien to their culture, and hence forced. It's a question of their being where they want to be because they choose to be there, not because the boss is watching them with a menacing look on his face. They made the decision and they are focused, attentive, connected and mindful.

To achieve this you will have to put up with, or even come to appreciate, their rites of connection (from going outside to smoke a cigarette, checking their Facebook account for ten minutes before starting work or during breaks, sipping coffee while staring out the window, playing music, sending personal emails for a minute or two, planning how they can do what they are about to do better, etc.). To each his own, as in Sinatra's song: I did it my way.

When the managers are performing their existential duties, they will also be at ease and not tempted to stand over anyone, aware that all the members of the company are necessary where they are and to the extent of their abilities. Everybody contributes, everybody works and everybody is travelling in the same vessel. Spirituality in business, experienced by each individual in his or her own way and not necessarily connected with any religion, has the effect of increasing the feeling of belonging to something bigger than yourself, of gratitude for what has been received and of satisfaction for work well done. There is no better attitude in life and no better work environment.

05
The Creative Ecosystem.
Third Factor: the Leadership and
Management Style

1. Aspects of the New Leadership

Contrary to what many people think, innovation is not the exclusive responsibility of the R&D department, nor that of the Director of Innovation. It is the responsibility of the entire team. This means that the kind of manager who was content to leave things as they were will now find himself under pressure. "Everything worked OK until now," used to be a good excuse, but it no longer works.

Companies where the management team has a superficial commitment, where it knows neither how to listen to nor manage the ideas put forward by its teams, and where new ideas are demanded without the necessary resources being provided, will never succeed in unchaining the innovative process with any degree of fluidity. In these organizations the creative impulse, the spark that generates the energy which brings coveted innovations along with it, is extinguished. In companies like this, however much they may invest in encouraging innovation, the result will always be the same: tending towards zero.

These changing times require new leaders who know how to unfold innovation so that its process is spread throughout the company. They will also have to learn to transform themselves into effective managers of the creative capital available, encouraging and rewarding those members of their team who decide to participate,

What are the keys of this new leadership? How is all the creative potential to be extracted? How is it to be efficiently managed? As a starting-point, a good leader should supply the resources (Re) needed for innovation, outstanding among which are time, training and, naturally, finance. He must also act as a catalysing vehicle to ensure that these resources turn into profitable ideas. In order to achieve this, he will have to manage his teams by placing special focus on three factors: communication (C), autonomy (A) and recognition and reward (R). If you wish or need to memorise this and build it into your routine, here is a simple mnemonic: Re-CAR.

Figure 5.1 Leadership and Management Style Factors

Resources (Re)

To innovate, resources are needed. At a minimum, this means time, training and finance. This is the foundation, and if any of the ingredients are lacking, it is unlikely that ideas will be generated.

Time is always short; it is limited and limiting. It is a non-elastic resource; perishable, non-storable and non-interchangeable. It is the most valuable resource there is; at least it is for many of us.

Unfortunately, it is also one of the main causes of anxiety and stress in life. The result of this has been that time and time management have been subjects of great interest since antiquity.

Time, both your own and that of others, is an essential feature in management science. When insufficient time is available, stress increases, initially as a motivational factor, but as time passes it become negative, exhausting and demotivating. The writer Peter Drucker summed it up very well, "Time is the scarcest resource in existence, and if it is not well managed, then nothing will be well managed." This means that the first thing a good leader must do is ensure that they use their own time efficiently. Time should be devoted to tasks that contribute value. This means that leadership styles that are based on orders and supervision should be abandoned, and leadership by example, which the modern era demands, should be the goal. Those who achieve this will be more effective and efficient, and they will also significantly improve the quality of their lives (less stress and more leisure), which will be much appreciated by their families and indeed their own bodies.

There is no consensus as to how a team's time should be managed. Many people fall back on approaches that are more connected with project management to achieve it. Adopting this course, they use deadlines and time pressure to achieve set goals. Sometimes this can be helpful, but it can also cause paralysis.

If deadlines are overrun and goals begin to feel just out of reach, isn't it likely that intentions will become lost? At a minimum, there will be the temptation to let things go, so goals must be handled with intelligence and thought of as challenges, rather than sanction-backed threats.

In the world of innovation, time is a basic resource. Innovators need time to think and leeway to sidestep reality. And yet time is also a limited and limiting resource, which gives rise to a difficult dilemma: how to achieve a profitable balance between the output from a traditional role (the day-to-day routine) and developing innovative potential? Or, put very simply, how much time do you devote to thinking, and how much to working?

We have all heard a great deal about Google's generosity in this field. Often it is held up as an example of how it is done. Google provided its employees with time to think and even time to develop their own projects. In some countries this occupied as much as 20 per cent of the working day. For most companies, such amount of time is probably excessive but some amount of time must be dedicated.

The second resource is training, an essential catalyst for transforming creative energy into new ideas. Creative and motivated people can only transform their innovative impulses into something tangible if they are well trained. Naturally, training in how to innovate may help, but it is important to go to the heart of the matter. Employees need proper training to perform day-to-day routine duties. This will also help them to understand how their job fits into the overall mechanism. It will be the duty of the management team and each one of its members to detect when training measures need to be put into action. The idea is to prevent a creativity leak from happening.

And we conclude with a few comments about finance. Innovation is not the direct fruit of budget allocations. This emphasises the fact that this is an essentially human process, but it does not imply that the budget is not essential. In those cases where the need for corrective action is detected (improving the information and communications network training actions, etc.), a fresh budget allocation is clearly required. And in a similar vein, time set aside for thinking involves a clear opportunity cost for the business. These are all essential investments.

Communication (C)

This is the term that represents the process by which the transmission of information and knowledge is achieved. It is a factor with an enormous effect on human activities, and there is no doubt that the innovation process is not unaffected by it.

Communication is the channel for transmitting strategy and business plans. Fluent and open communication stimulates commitment to the corporate identity and mission, and helps it consolidate and develop. It is also an essential tool for generating the organization culture, climate and image. When communication flows, it generates an atmosphere of trust that boosts motivation and can even awaken corporate enthusiasm, but it also exercises a great deal of influence on the quality of life and happiness scale in the workplace. Put simply, it is essential for the actual functioning of a company.

However, it is not always easy to manage. Communication takes place via verbal and non-verbal signals, and implies a significant degree of complexity. Indeed, many researchers hold that non-verbal language is the most important aspect of the process. The result is that today's company leaders face the difficult necessity of learning to manage not only what is objective, but also what is subjective.

Particularly well known in this field are the experiments carried out by psychologist Albert Mehrabian (1972). His research gave rise to the famous 7-38-55 rule, according to which seven per cent of a message we receive comes from words, while the rest derives from the tone of voice (38 per cent) and body language (55 per cent).

Research in the same field conducted by anthropologist Raymond Birdwhistell (1970), produced rather less dramatic figures. According to him, some 35 per cent of communications derives from verbal content, while the remaining 65 per cent is the product of body language. In both cases the findings are the results of laboratory work, which has often been poorly interpreted (or too rigidly interpreted), but that nonetheless clearly pointed out the importance of non-verbal communication, and hence the complexity involved with managing such communication.

Companies keen to make their mark in the world of innovation must strive to include leaders capable of stimulating satisfactory communication among both in-house and external levels within their management team. Those who manage this will have succeeded in implementing the most effective mechanism in existence for tackling the worst enemy of organizational creativity: resistance to change.

No universal rule exists to explain how to deploy such networks successfully. Each individual organization will have to set up its own communication system to include both informal and formal systems within its management. A network will have to be established to ensure that all the members of an organization are kept informed, and that also ensures that they, too, can communicate. It will need to be a two-way channel, capable of transmitting messages and also watching out for concerns, suggestions and recommendations from all levels. This is the only way commitment can be expected from each and every employee.

Autonomy (A)

Autonomy can be defined as the condition whereby, as far as certain matters are concerned, an individual is dependent on no one. This concept reflects the level of freedom that allows an individual to plan his or her work and decide upon the methods for carrying it out. There is no doubt that it exercises a powerful influence on our commitment, motivation and behaviour. No great detail is required to explain its effect. How many of you would feel motivated if you were told exactly what you had to do, how and when to do it, with no room for your own input or opinion? Very few, to be sure, and I would not be among you.

Deci and Ryan's psychological theory of Self-Determination (1985) clearly explains its effects in a number of fields, such as sport, for example. According to these researchers our behaviour is governed by two types of innate needs: physiological needs, such as hunger or thirst and psychological needs, which, along with autonomy, include factors such as social relationships and competition.

This theory states that everyone needs to be able to choose between different options. This is a requisite for feeling motivated, and when it's not met, sooner or later you become demotivated. This means that professionals responsible for teams must ensure that their workers are permitted the appropriate degree of autonomy. It is, of course, no easy matter for "leaders" who are accustomed to doing precisely that – organising matters so that their teams do things because they are told to. A 180-degree about-face is required in their management style.

There is no doubt that allowing the workforce a significant degree of self-management and autonomy carries risks. Each team member must understand how his or her work fits into the big picture for it to be successful. And it demands that each individual accept responsibility, make commitments, understand how to organize him or herself, and of course, work in a team. In this context, autonomy is not isolation; it is a form of empowerment that allows each worker to give his or her best as an individual, but also as a member of a team, such that synergies can be sought from the total effort. No other kind of action is possible in the world of open innovation.

Autonomy creates challenges, and gives rise to much more in the way of opportunities. In other words, it is necessary and the risk is worth the cost. With greater autonomy you are more productive and innovative, and you're also happier. That is something which is not only contagious, but also profitable, with an extremely desirable multiplier effect.

Recognition and Reward (R)

Failure is a word greatly feared in the world of business. Self-esteem is in danger every time you fail. It may become a burden, paralysing and frustrating you; it may even become a stigma. And yet, it also has a positive angle and can be very profitable. With the right attitude it can strengthen and teach you. The important thing is to know how to face it and get up again after a fall. Failure is generally much more instructive than success. With the right attitude, each failure is followed by a period of reflection that reveals mistakes made. Those who know how to do this end up proud of their defeats, their war wounds.

Winston Churchill put it very succinctly, "Success is not final, failure is not fatal: it is the courage to continue that counts." It is part of the journey and necessary for learning something new. Even so, leaving your comfort zone is risky. This means that leaders who wish to harvest their teams' maximum creative potential will have to support and even publicly reward the daring and courage of those who step out of their comfort zones and take chances that could lead to failure.

The word "publicly" is very important. If the reward is not visible, it will have much less impact, only affecting the recipient.

When reward is visible to others and when recognition is public, it produces a multiplier effect that extends to include the full team.

Of course, not all failures should be rewarded. Rewards should go to those who risk something (reputation, etc.) to achieve a difficult but valuable goal. Consequently, programmes must be established that acknowledge successes and reward intelligent failures from which all can learn.

How can this be achieved? To design an effective recognition and reward plan, a plan that motivates people, requires an excellent understanding of human psychology – of people's needs and desires. It is not sufficient to understand how groups function. Individual qualities must also be acknowledged. To begin with, a good knowledge of available motivational mechanisms is required.

Fortunately, financial rewards are not the only motivational tools available. Professional prestige can also be a significant lever. It is a fact that most people need to have their efforts acknowledged. This means that public rewards involving actions that stimulate prestige are usually very effective. Each company and each manager must develop their own formula.

Companies keen on being leading innovators will have to hire leaders who oversee that the innovative machinery is operating at full tilt. They must provide the necessary resources, and they must also guarantee effective communications. They must permit and encourage autonomy as well, and provide desirable rewards and means of recognition.

We should not leave this section without adding a few lines about a subject that in reality should need no comment, yet which continues to be a problem in a great number of companies in the field of innovation, and a tough obstacle to the development of innovative potential: diversity management.

Diversity has a direct impact on the economic and financial yield of an organization. By way of example, worthy of mention is the study entitled *Diversity and Performance Report*. BMJ Ratings was commissioned by UNESCO to produce this report in 2009, and its conclusions left little room for doubt. It showed that sociocultural diversity were responsible for 49 per cent of variance in economic results for the 120 multinationals analysed. In other words, the research showed a strong causal connection and revealed that companies must implement necessary mechanisms to render their internal diversity as profitable as possible.

How can this be done? The traditional approach to diversity has been to concentrate on respecting individual differences of all people and all groups. This was a perception based on respect and tolerance in search of equality. It has evolved, however, and is now focused on treating individuals differently, according to their needs and circumstances. This is a qualitative step forward, stressing the fact that the contributions made by each of us must be optimised. This is a serious challenge, since moving from team management to the management of individuals is not easy, but the advantages can be very profitable.

2. Innova 3DX for Leadership and Management Style

Leadership and management style are normally responsible for between 10 – 20 per cent of innovative behaviour for both genders.

There is an interesting gender disparity given that women are frequently much more influenced by this factor than men. Companies where this is true should be very aware of it if they want to make the most of the both genders' innovative potentials.

How does it affect us? Here's an example: if your departmental manager is known to be against innovation and refuses to provide resources – does not allow training and requires you to meet impossible deadlines, how keen are you to be innovative? Do you even have time? The answer is obvious. Let's go a step further: if communication is minimal, if you feel you're being watched and that your efforts aren't rewarded, do you even *dare* to innovate?

Even so, its influence on your behaviour spreads, as it does in the case of corporate culture and work climate, via their impact on your potential and passion for innovation. How will an act of public recognition that rewards risk-taking innovation affect your self-esteem? Will you be afraid of failure in an environment that rewards intelligent failures? Put briefly, communication exercises a clear influence that works directly and indirectly.

Even so, what is most noticeable is its relationship with corporate culture and the work climate, where it may either act as a catalyst or have a neutralising effect. Let's assume that the culture and climate of the company encourage us to be innovative, but the boss is a self-confessed anti-innovator. How many of you will take a chance? I suspect very few. Naturally, there will always be exceptions, and risks are possible, but if it's going to cause problems, maybe we should devote our precious creativity to some less dangerous task.

In short, this factor may be a great accelerant in a positive culture with a satisfactory work climate, but it can be a dangerous obstacle in other circumstances. Yet very few companies attach the same importance to these other two factors or monitor them regularly and systematically. Those keen to shine in this field must keep this in the forefront of their minds.

Figure 5.2 Leadership and Management Style Test

Given that the goal of the first dimension is to provide a picture of the innovation levers and obstacles from the viewpoint of the ecosystem, this test will measure the leadership and management style surrounding the person answering the test. For those managing teams, this test can also stand as a valuable tool for measuring their own leadership style. It will provide very useful information for continuing along the inno-leadership route.

Instructions: give a score for your opinion on each statement on a scale from 0 – 10, with 0 as the lowest score and 10 the highest. You may use decimals if you wish.

Resources (Re)		
1.	I have time to think.	— —, —
2.	I have all the time I need to do my work well.	— —, —
3.	I have all the training I need to do my work well.	— —, —
4.	I have all the resources I need to do my work well.	— —, —
5.	I have the economic resources I need to do my work well.	— —, —
Average score		— —, —
Communication (C)		
1.	Communication with my boss is fluent.	— —, —
2.	I can communicate with my boss any time I want to.	— —, —
3.	My boss keeps me directly informed about anything happening in the company.	— —, —
4.	My boss keeps me continually informed about anything happening in the company.	— —, —

5.	I can express myself freely.	— —, —
Average score		— —, —

Autonomy (A)

1.	I am involved in defining the content of my work.	— —, —
2.	I am involved in my planning.	— —, —
3.	I feel quite autonomous in my day-to-day routine.	— —, —
4.	My boss allows me all the autonomy I need.	— —, —
5.	I feel that I have all the leeway I need to take decisions about my day-to-day routine.	— —, —
Average score		— —, —

Rewards (R)

1.	My boss rewards success.	— —, —
2.	My boss rewards what's courageous.	— —, —
3.	My boss knows how to acknowledge work that is done well.	— —, —
4.	My boss is able to publicly acknowledge work done well.	— —, —
5.	I feel that my boss recognizes the quality of my work.	— —, —
Average score		— —, —

Result: from 0 – 3.5 (inclusive) very low, from 3.5 – 5 (inclusive) low, from 5 – 6.5 (inclusive) satisfactory, from 6.5 – 10 (inclusive) very high.

What kinds of leadership and management style govern your day-to-day routine? To answer, insert the averages obtained from the measurement test into the following table.

Figure 5.3 Leadership and Management Style Factor Table

Resources	Communication	Autonomy	Reward

Managers who provide no resources and who do not communicate – neither allowing autonomy nor giving rewards are destroyers of creativity. Not only do they fail to facilitate the creative process, they also marshal all their competitive energy to ensure that the innovative impulse is extinguished. For this reason I refer to them as "innovation killers".

On the other side of the fence are managers who do provide resources and manage all the factors with great effectiveness. These are the inno-leaders who intelligently catalyse the creative energy of their teams in order to generate valuable ideas.

And of course, between these two extremes are all those managers who tread the highway of this new leadership road. These professionals have to work out the areas in need of improvement and develop them until they can join the inno-leaders group. Those who succeed are ready to start creating the future.

3. Insight Management and Leadership Style

Many people have managed to misinterpret the well-known *The Art of War* by the fourth century Chinese author, Sun Tzu, and in transporting it to the 21st century, misunderstood it as advocating a warlike management style, encouraging corporate violence from within and without. This is a poor reading of this work, since if you actually understood it, you'd see that it's a masterpiece of strategy and careful analysis which when well applied, means that most battles can be avoided. As the legend states, two Samurai warriors were about to cross a river, each from the opposite end of a bridge, and when they met, they each gripped their swords and looked long into each others' eyes without fighting, until at last, one realized that the other was the superior warrior, and continued on his way along the river, without offering resistance.

Unfortunately we are not so well prepared, having neither the sensitivity nor the well-polished self-awareness, so we hurl ourselves into savage battles to test what could be worked out without violence or death – either our own or that of others. To prepare for the battle that should not be fought, we need only to carefully interpret Sun Tzu and take another step forward. The work of multidimensional insight management can be accomplished with the help of yet another ancient master, Lao Tzu, acknowledged writer of the *Tao Te Ching* in the 4th century BC:

> The Heavens are eternal and the Earth remains because they do not exist for themselves, but give themselves over to the One. In the same way, the sage puts himself behind, yet always finds himself to the fore, because by setting aside his own interests, he finds them realized all the more greatly. They never leave the One, and hence realize the integrity of their Being.

Thanks to the teachings of this old master we realize that we are all much more connected than we thought, and although we have different paths to follow, we all form part of the same phenomenon, the same energy, One, Tao or whatever else we may wish to call it. We all belong to the same genius. In this light it's easier to understand such multidimensional subjects as the individual, labour relations, creativity, innovation, motivation, success, passion, good governance, and feelings of belonging, etc.

In other words, you could continue to see reality as a bloody battleground with workers and companies facing each other in a comic Sun Tzu version, or you could play in another league by observing the harmony that exists behind chaos and understand, or at least acknowledge, universal order. You could experience individual and group energy, real fulfilment, being in a creative vacuum, receiving the support and profound respect of co-workers and managers. This would make it easier for each individual to develop their own new business model, career, life and happiness – which would be ever changing, eternal and fluid.

Let's return to the here and now with realism in our hearts, a concept created 2,500 years ago as the only valid starting-point for work. The world of business continues to be in the hands of authoritarian management, glass ceilings, a hostile climate and the murder of entrepreneurship and creativity. The first serious mistake would be to create an authority that cannot be questioned, that serves to impose order, but not necessarily for the right reason. In addition, although the authority argument is very convenient for the unquestioned superior, the phenomenology of many a crisis reveals the obvious. You'd better think about it twice, before starting a war.

The manager, or it might be better to say the person that the company now needs, must deploy his own unique way of seeing and acting in order to get the best from himself and his team. He must know himself in order to flow with changing realities. He will have to work on himself in order to understand what state reality is in at any given moment, to pull away the veil that clouds perception. Awareness will help him, not only to see well, but to travel lightly in order to travel further – as a person, part of a team or a project or company etc. Whatever doesn't add, takes away. To sum up he must be daring, ambitious, nonconformist, ready to leave his comfort zone, able to be creative as a team member and always keen to learn and be prepared for exposure to a variety of stimuli.

"Empty of dogma and doctrine, the cup of wisdom will never overflow."

Tao Te Ching

By developing themselves they become sages, people who know themselves and recognize each other in the members of the team, not just knowing each others' names, but knowing *who* they actually are, what they are into and what they can offer at any passing moment. Managers and individuals who become like this can humbly facilitate procedures in such a way that their talent is used to the maximum. They can tirelessly support, help, encourage and confront without prejudice. These are the people who are capable of constructing genuine relationships, listening, learning and who generate amazement. In their company, everything flows, everything grows, and nothing is constrained by ceilings or walls made of glass.

The required style of leadership has changed. Before the second world war, fascist politics dragged their countries up from their profound economic and ideological depressions, albeit temporarily, thanks to the Führer or the Duce. These huge personalities led the masses who blindly followed them and never broke step, directing all their energy towards the same goal. Modern times, call for new and urgent measures, in both the private and public spheres. The temptation to go back to authoritarian leadership is there again, but we must fully register these lessons from history, in order not to make the same mistakes.

Today' leaders must be sensitive, capable of reading others' needs, potential and creative energy, but above all, they must facilitate movement. Instead of imposing a generic order, diversity must be enhanced, along with each individual's unique character via their unique resources. Energy streams must be followed, not dammed. This means that the leader's position is no longer at the head as in the past, but behind – or in the midst – in contact with available resources, observing changes, and facilitating or even boosting them.

Speaking of travelling in the midst reminds me of an advertisement that showed people inside separate individually coloured bubbles. When they reached the underground station, they all squeezed against each other until they reached a kind of limit. Far from giving me the impression of exhaustion, I felt that it seemed much safer to travel this way, leaning against each other, bumping, jostling and pressing. Modern physics says we live in a much emptier world than we thought and should take advantage of it. Our obsession with concentrating on what is under our noses rather than the space around it, and on our individuality in a competitive society, is doing us no favours. If we were not so concentrated on our own issues and on comparing ourselves with others we would fearlessly express our genius in a way that would encourage others.

I had a businessman client working in Moscow who urgently consulted me on Skype because his company was planning to have him subjected to an external psychological examination to assess whether he would be able to handle a particular project. His initial reaction was fear, naturally, as most people assume they're not good enough, and his first request was for me to supply him with foolproof answers so that he could come out ahead. I don't judge him, this happens to us all sooner or later. Actually we are taught to do it since we are little, getting the wrong impression that we are not good enough, therefore we have to be somebody else, in order to be successful – in other words, spending energy in this direction freezes the imagination, perverts your nature, cripples the individual and robs you of your individuality, creativity and potential.

Managers must learn to understand both the effect and the power of emotions, their own and those of others. Emotions are temporary and must always be monitored. I have had clients who have confessed to a total incapability of understanding anything on an emotional level, whether regarding themselves or their families. They always want to escape back to the office, to the respect paid to them by their subordinates because of their high positions. Those who have achieved this status through emotional sacrifice, self-pressure and holding their breath can no longer understand nor tolerate anything else.

But those who would also like to extract the totality of creative potential from their teams must understand that creativity is not a straightforward process – steps forward and backward must be made in order to advance. Creating and destroying. Relaxing and tensing. Managers are frequently found urging their people on to ever greater efforts, when what their people need is to do nothing at all and soak themselves in fertile emptiness, maybe even *undo* some things. There's virtue in taking no action, passing no judgement and simply observing what emerges in due course.

> "The sea is the king of the streams and rivers because it is beneath them."
>
> *Tao Te Ching*

It is essential to allow people to set free their creative energy, and in order to achieve that, the best thing to do is humbly withdraw following the principle of non-intervention. If you must get involved, then try being an observer: non-judgemental, simply hoping for the best. The ugly duckling turns into a swan, and the wonderful *homo sapiens* as a new-born baby is a monkey who looks like a very old person, adored by the parents, but whom many of the hospital visitors battle to see as anything but simply ugly. In art the red-haired madman who sold nothing turns out to be the genius Van Gogh, and the pariah Toulouse-Lautrec was, after all, an eternal innovator

Talent is hard to recognize, and the entrepreneurial and creative spirit is often quashed by a superior afraid of being eclipsed. This fact has resulted in many countries suffering the worst talent drain in their histories. Public and private institutions, together with managers, must learn to appreciate, encourage, recognize and reward those who step out of their comfort zones to take on personal and professional risks. That would help to make the quantum leap that we all need and for which we have invested so much and for so long.

When you're very full, there's no room for anything: you have to empty yourself in order to be able to learn. People who have been very successful and then fail have to reset their objectives, get back to basics, dump their baggage and trust that their old genius will come back to look after them and provide fresh new successes. But if they do it according to the old system, the likelihood is that they will never come out ahead again, since everything is in constant movement.

If emptiness is more important than fullness, why are you training? What is the minimum necessary? It's a fact that a graphic designer absolutely must be in charge of his tools in order to be able to express his creativity. So far, we are in agreement. But now let me slightly upset all those people who never see themselves as "good enough" and always assume that they need more training and experience in order to give the best of themselves. This kind of imaginary shortfall is a huge obstacle to the creative process. It deceives you and everybody else. Get trained because you want to; perfect excellence but not because you lack training and are no good without it. Remember that you used to be a child once, and felt permitted to play with your creativity and explore it, but then you got trained and learnt what others did with their creativity. Now that you've grown up you need to go back to being a child again and discard the models of excellence that shimmer in your retina and dare to make your own way. If you don't, you'll never be more than a copier, and however brilliant a copier you are – and some are brilliant – you will never be better than the original, because copies contribute nothing new. This may seem like a trite platitude, but when most of us set out to create and innovate, we tend to do so on the basis of a previous creation, yet when we sink into deep thought we can imagine that we're capable of resurfacing with real gems to show to the world. We imagine that we can express our uniqueness, and that separates us or the firm from the rest.

Now that the information storm is in overdrive, information can easily turn into noise, and to add to the information further as part of a strategy might be a very expensive mistake. Your ears and your ability to digest the information are already swamped. So choose the essential information very carefully; choose what needs to be distributed. The world is full of detailed reports that somebody commissioned but in the end, nobody reads. So be practical. Less is more, or, at least, more is not always more, and often it is less. Carefully examine what you are going to communicate and decide whether it's just noise. Is it of interest to the recipient? Is it just you showing off?

Demagogues and strangers to the deeper paths may think that so much emptiness provides the grounds for taking it easy, slowing down the rhythm, productivity and attention, but they are seriously wrong. We are talking about training powerful people, not limp victims.

A typical example of a victim is someone who says, "They never give me any time." Naturally. Nobody gives anybody any time. Time is simply a guide. In a technological life where parameters are constantly changing, the actual limits, which are time, space and money, become something essential.

If Peter Drucker is right, and "time is the scarcest resource in existence", it's paradoxical that most people behave as though their lives were infinite, with little attention paid to what is important, and all attention focused on what is urgent right now, with the result that their lives pass without important things getting done; the important things being those things they really *wanted* to do, both personally and professionally.

Shamans urge us to see death as our companion, always at your side in the car, in the train, when you travel or take a stroll; with the knowledge of death always present, you live your life knowing it is finite. Poor readings of the culturally closer *carpe diem,* which actually turns out to be the same thing, encourage excessive time and energy wasting as mere existential alleviation. And yet, being aware of death and the limitations of time helps you to prioritise, focus, activate and develop a day that has shape; where nothing is superfluous, everything has significance – and production and creation have their own space, just the way affection does. Those who fail to learn this lesson commit to staying at work while nobody is left in the office and they still complain that they are short of time. To make matters worse, they do so thinking that it will improve their jobs or careers. If you're the boss in this case, and the task matches the time available, don't let them play these games: please tell them to go home.

06
Innovative Potential. First Factor: Creativity

1. Background and Discussion

Innovation and creativity are two very similar concepts, so intimately interwoven that you can find plenty of people writing about them as though they meant the same thing, but they do not. So I shall begin by clarifying their meanings.

An innovation is the outcome of an idea (a new creative contribution) with an application and an entry into the market. In comparison, creativity is "the faculty of creation or the capacity to create". The difference between the two is therefore the possible profitability of an idea. The demarcation is blurred, given that the application of this rule is not always easy, but what matters is to understand the essence of the difference.

The word creativity derives from the Latin *creare,* which means both to produce and to create. It means to cause something to be that had not previously existed. Historically it has been a synonym for genius, originality, inventiveness, discovery and even productivity. In the world of psychology it has been likened to the terms fantasy and imagination.

It is a natural aspect of all human beings. Neuroscience states that creativity is generated in the right hemisphere of the brain, which also contains artistic expression, affection and sense of fun. In other words, we are all creative; we are all capable of creating. The differentiating factor is in the level of creative potential each of us possesses. This means that people who think that it is a quality found in only a few privileged souls are wrong.

This leads to an old question that is still of interest: what makes some people more creative than others? Many different answers have been suggested, none of which receive universal agreement, although a common factor might be that most explanations assume that a genetic creative nature can be developed via suitable techniques. These tools can apparently release a new thought process that is complementary to the processor-type reasoning stimulated by traditional educational systems through disciplines such as mathematics or statistics.

Among these tools are a number of techniques that work individually, such as the mental maps described by Tony Buzan (1996), who is an expert on the workings of the brain. Buzan's proposed technique suggests graphic representations and mental mapping to boost cerebral capacity for learning and processing information. In more concrete terms, he presents these maps as a tool to represent normally abstract mental processes via shapes, colours and dimensions. The result is that it allows the free expression of the emotions, stimulates the imagination and combines ideas to generate fresh ones. According to the author, this is a technique that stimulates both sides of the brain so that it can harvest the totality of our creative potential.

De Bono (1985), creator of the term "lateral thinking", suggests a technique that he calls the six hats method. This tool, invented to generate debate, discussion and decision-making, is based on disentangling thought processes by separating them into elements such as the emotions, information, logic, hope and creativity.

As with individual techniques, group dynamics are also powerful. For over 400 years a method has been used to seek new pathways for "problems without solutions". Known as *Prai-Barshana,* where *prai* means outside of yourself and *barshana* means question, it operates as a form of collective catharsis. The participants form a circle from which new thoughts are called forth, in an environment where there are no standards or limitations, and in which there is no leeway for destructive criticism.

Because this method seemed to work, it was exported to New York where it was further developed until it became known as "brainstorming". This methodology is now seen as an essential technique, one that is very effective for producing ideas among a group. It is effective as long as the imagination is completely untrammelled and critical judgement is suspended.

Role-playing is also very effective. This is a tool that works with experimentation, so that many people see it as the same as a social psychology laboratory. Half a century ago *The Wall Street Journal* accurately described the essence of the technique, "It provides an actor with a perception of the viewpoints of other people when they play the role of others, whether on the stage or in real life."

Naturally, there are other tools. We find, for example, the SCAMPER method (a technique based on a new idea-generating checklist) and the "waking dreaming" approach (derived from the therapeutic area). All offer a range of different results and huge potential for companies and professionals who are determined to innovate. A crucial player in the history of creativity is Joy Paul Guilford, former president of the American Psychological Association. At a key conference in 1950, Guilford expressed his consternation at the indifference and lack of interest concerning the matter, especially as far as psychology was concerned, with the result that the term "creativity" became a regular reference in this discipline. Until that time, literature and research in this area had concentrated on intelligence and its relationship with creativity.

For Guilford (1985), intelligent people are those who can work out a solution to a given problem using data and knowledge, logic and experience. This is what is known as convergent thinking. By comparison, creative people are able to produce original responses using associations or imagination that are different from those that would've been arrived at using convergent ratiocination. These people are using divergent thinking. According to this definition, the intelligent process is divergent by nature, while creation is expansive. In other words, the difference between both types of thinking is found in the breaking of limits, with intelligence remaining within the structures of knowledge, and creativity managing to breach these barriers. By contrast, according to Robert J. Sternberg (1988), professor and researcher at Yale University, creativity is found within the construct of human intelligence. Within his Triarchic Theory he includes three types of intelligence: analytical, practical and creative.

These are just a sample of the opinions expressed in the debate about the relationship between intelligence and creativity; many more exist. Indeed, interesting research continues to be made in this field with an eye to seeking consensus. In any case, there is no doubt that a high level of creativity calls for a certain threshold of intelligence, which is fundamental for creative solutions to add value.

Since the actions open to a company are normally aimed at measuring and improving the creativity and not the intelligence of staff and contractors, we shall focus on this factor. Naturally, this does not mean that intelligence is not important, but we shall adopt the approach that regards it as the basis of creativity.

The relationship between intelligence, creativity and gender continues to be a fruitful source of polemic. Far from new, the debate has been current for centuries and is no less energetic at the present time. For the most part it has adopted an androcentric viewpoint that has stigmatised the feminine, in general, in the fields of intelligence *and* creativity.

The research carried out by Jonsson and Carlsson (2000) is very interesting as it analyses the relationship between sex and creativity, and notes that individuals who score high on creativity also scored high in both masculine and feminine areas at the same time (androgyny), or to the contrary scored low (undifferentiated) on both. This is known as psychological androgyny. However, let's approach the question directly. Are men or women more intelligent and/or creative? In order to respond let's take a short historical survey of some of the opinions expressed, but first, I want to highlight that creativity as a concept began to generate interest in the 1950s, which means that until that time, the literature available concentrated on intelligence – which will therefore have to be the main focus of this survey.

Huarte de San Juan (1530-1589) provides what is for many people the first psychological theory of gender difference in his work, translated as *The Examination of Men's Wits* or *The Examination of Talents for the Professions*. The author bases his work on the bodily humours (the liquids in the human body). According to his theory, the masculine temperament can be defined as the heat/dryness dichotomy, while the feminine is defined by the cold/moist pairing. In the opinion of the writer, intelligence needs dryness, something that is maintained by the testicles, and the reason behind the fact that men are intrinsically more intelligent than women.

He also offers profound considerations such as, "parents who wish to enjoy the pleasure of wise children – children skilled in their letters – have striven to produce boys; because girls, due to the coolness and moistness of their sex, are unable to develop great intelligence. We see that they speak with the appearance of intelligence in light and trivial matters, using common and frequently heard terms, but when it comes to the study of letters they are unable to learn more than a little Latin, and this they do solely by rote. They are not to blame, as it is the coldness and moistness that has made them female. We have already proven that these same qualities run counter to intelligence and ability."

Freud (1930) similarly confirmed in his essay *Civilization and Its Discontents*, that sublimation is found to a lesser extent in women, which limits their artistic and intellectual output. His opinion was obvious with remarks such as, "the following discord is caused by women, who are not slow to oppose the cultural current, exercising their dilatory and conservative influence [...]. Women represent the interests of the family and sexual life; cultural work, however, is increasingly a masculine concern, imposing increasing difficulties on men and obliging them to sublimate their instincts, a sublimation which women are ill able to offer."

Likewise, the disputed but famous German neurologist Paul Julius Moebius, in his work *On the Physiological Mental Deficiency of Woman* (1898), stated that in animals, intelligence is inversely proportional to fecundity, which proved that women were less intelligent than men, since they were biologically dedicated to procreation.

I feel sure that many readers will feel that the distance in time, in terms of these works, explains the opinions offered, and simply assume they can no longer be defended. They will believe that they are only of historical value, and yet this is not the case. It is very far from it. For this reason I cannot conclude this section without glancing at recent opinions of other researchers and experts from a variety of disciplines who have made similar statements.

An interesting and controversial work on the subject of gender and intelligence work was published in 2005 by Paul Irwing of Manchester University and Richard Lynn of Ulster University in the *British Journal of Psychology*. The study states that adult women have a lower IQ than their male companions, which affects their prosperity. Curiously, for these researchers, the actual size of the brain matters (male brains are 10 per cent bigger than female ones), which is a factor in determining the level of intelligence of each sex.

And following the same path, but now with a focus on creativity, I should mention the work *Genius and Madness* by Philippe Brenot (2000). According to this French psychiatrist and anthropologist, who also happens to be the president of the International Observatory of the Couple: "A genius is a man."

Of course, these are exceptions, given that this type of opinion is increasingly rare (at least when in the public arena) and they are seen as at the least, unreliable. Even so, they are still found largely because of the serious media impact wielded by their authors. This could provoke negative psychological effects on the men and women who read their opinions.

2. Innova 3DX for Creativity

Creativity alone is responsible for between 15 – 25 per cent of the innovative behaviour of men and women. This figure shows the need to monitor this quality and do what is needed to ensure 100 per cent expression.

Those aiming to develop and maximise their innovative potential or that of their teams must understand that creativity does not exist within us in isolation. We will be unable to really develop it unless we have a wider picture of the situation. We need to remember that it is intrinsically connected with our psychological traits, and no matter how hard we strive to express the totality of our creative potential, if we are lax we shall effectively hit the brakes on its development. For example, let's take a look at the relationship between optimism and self-esteem.

To dispel the fog of uncertainty surrounding innovation requires a touch of optimism. An optimist sees possibilities and advantages in ideas that a pessimist immediately discards.

An optimist also sees challenges more positively and accesses greater strength for confronting them.

However, the benefits go much further than that. Optimists experience lower stress levels, are more relaxed than pessimists, are more connected to their environment and are therefore more likely to come up with ideas. In short, they are more receptive and fertile. This individual creativity can also be quite inspiring and boost the imaginations of the other team members. In other words, we have to be optimists, regardless of the circumstances. It will make it easier for us to find the energy and strength needed to locate new pathways and overcome the obstacles that may arise. This means that optimism is an important personal and business asset.

Self-esteem is also closely associated with innovation. To deploy all our creativity in the face of the risks involved, we must trust in our ability and strength to achieve results. If that confidence is absent, ideas fade quickly. Of course, it is possible for people with low self-esteem to display creativity once in a while, but they will lack the power to convert it into something profitable. As a result, a company that acts to erode the self-esteem of its teams is moving along a path to destruction.

Figure 6.1 Creativity Test

We all possess creative potential and it can be developed using appropriate techniques. Very few people are able to draw on 100 per cent of the creative capacity within them. The main aim of this test is to help detect the possible existence of those self-imposed creativity blocks. Naturally, actions designed to boost entrepreneurial genius may attack both pathways (potential and blocks), but we recommend starting with the second, since in the alternative case, creativity leaks may neutralise efforts made to develop individual potential.

Instructions: score your opinion on each statement from 0 – 10, with 0 as the lowest score and 10 the highest. You may use decimals if you wish.

1.	I have many ideas.	___ ___ , ___
2.	I have good ideas.	___ ___ , ___
3.	I have a good imagination.	___ ___ , ___
4.	I see myself as a creative individual.	___ ___ , ___
5.	Other people see me as creative.	___ ___ , ___
Average score		___ ___ , ___

Result: from 0 – 3.5 (inclusive) very low, from 3.5 – 5 (inclusive) low, from 5 – 6.5 (inclusive) adequate, from 6.5 – 10 (inclusive) very high.

Are you a builder of new realities (a divergent thinker), or do you feel more at home among those who feel incapable of doing this, or who don't function that way (non-divergent thinkers)? Creativity is essential for those who are banking on entrepreneurship as a way of life; for those who need to reinvent themselves and reinvent their business in an ever-changing world. But it is not just important for them. In the world of open innovation, where everybody takes part, business must hone its collective genius, and that means that every one of us will be called upon to deploy our 100 per cent. Don't raise your own limits – bank on creativity.

3. Insight Management and Creativity

Just jot down here your desires without using any criteria. Write them, use photographs, make a collage, or you can even paint them if you want.

Then here write how you would achieve those dreams, how you would turn them into reality.

And now write down all the criticisms you can think of about what you've put above. Ignore how harsh they seem.

Did you complete the exercise? If the answer is no, you're making a big mistake thinking that reading about creativity is going to boost yours. Go back to page one, have dreams and work to achieve them. It will do you – and everybody around you – good.

Now you've completed it? Good, congratulations. Now you have to give some thought to what you're doing in your life to turn it into reality. What actual steps are you taking? Write them down on another page – you don't get let off the hook so easily! What are you doing to prevent anything from happening (write it)? And when you've finished, read it through, think about it, keep these handwritten pages, turn them into a mural where you can see them, examine them, add to or edit them from time to time. Awareness will give wings to your creative power, perfecting your sense of the mission and hence your feelings of existential, personal and professional satisfaction and happiness.

Creativity has been sought after and facilitated by any number of techniques over the years, from the practices of yoga, Taoism and Zen Buddhism – from the ancients up to the most modern of humanistic psychotherapies, such as Gestalt, or NLP (neuro-linguistic programming) with its famous Walt Disney technique. The exercise we've just witnessed with the blank sheets is a version of that, with a few additions.

All these techniques – as a general rule, and specifically with the Walt Disney system – include unlimited room for dreaming with divergent, chaotic and peripheral thinking that could include linear thinking, as well. There are no limits or rules, there's just creativity. You must dare to dream. And then you have to transform these dreams into reality in some way. How? Where? With what? By means of what actual steps? Many people become thoroughly frustrated, frozen at the dream stage – like children – never able to realize their dreams. Once you've had a dream, assess its viability, work out how it can be realized and create an opportunity for yourself to at least work out *how* to do it. I am frequently consulted by people who talk to me about their profoundest and most longed-for dreams, like going on a mission to work in Africa, flying a plane or parachuting to the ground. Many need a travelling companion such as me, someone who, once they have worked out what the dreams are, will ask them how they are going to achieve this, until they answer with concrete steps, or until they give up the dream and allow it to be replaced by more realistic dreams that can genuinely be turned into reality.

Initially it is essential that both creator and observer be completely non-judgemental. This means that the first step is to give yourself permission to create without any prior judgements about your own capacity. Then if you've created what you dreamt about, take a good look at it. Don't judge the result and don't discard it before giving it some time. Wait, look at it, stop looking at it, and now look at it again. Add and subtract, place and remove, wait, contemplate, observe. You can start out thinking that you're going to paint a picture or creatively reorganise the storage system, as Zara's founder Amancio Ortega did in his time, and I quote: "I didn't know it couldn't be done." There are a great many fields of activity, indeed they are unlimited, if you don't construct limits. Naturally, if you decide to work on a 10 x 10 cm canvas, you know you can't go outside of it.

The final step is to invite the critic. Is there anything missing? Does this make sense in this framework? Can it be defended? Do we have the technology to develop this idea? Will it make a profit? In light of the productive and financial empire that resulted from Walt Disney's creativity, few would have the cheek to say that he was just some geezer with birds and mice in his head. Of course he was and of course he could dream, but he also had his feet on the ground and knew how to turn his creativity into very productive and innovative productions.

I would like to briefly mention my own speciality here: meditation techniques and mind-body work. In the residential workshops I hold, exercises such as the one we just performed take place at the very end of an intense weekend of working with the body, meditating, reducing the noise, deconstructing poses and automatic responses, and recovering energy, spontaneity and the freedom of being. All these terms – which seem so threatening to some people – are a wonderful gift for those who know how to receive them. Approaching creativity in the wake of these kinds of experience has little to do with the experience of an individual just sitting at home faced with a blank sheet of paper. Creating is not the same as creating after meditation. This is not just my praise for the effects of these techniques in the wake of 20 years of practice, nor is it that they are urged by some sadhu or loincloth-wearing guru emerging from a cave in India. The fact is that right now, these teachings are not only accessible by all, but highly acknowledged in the east and in the west, by practitioners and by researchers at universities such as California (Davis and San Francisco), Queensland, North Carolina (UNCC), Massachusetts, China (U. T. Dalian), Texas and Las Palmas in Spain's Canary Islands, among others.

All these and many others present rigorous arguments based on the evidence produced by techniques such as brain-imaging diagnosis, enzyme measurement, facts and figures for telomeres (the ends of the chromosomes), the sponginess of the brain, cortex and hippocampus, etc. Working with energy in general and meditation in particular helps avoid hippocampus wear and even supports regeneration, lowers stress, helps focus attention, boosts our sense of happiness and supports organism-focused self-regulation with direct effects on the cure of a thousand and one conditions. Moreover, meditation generates a mental and experiential space within which creativity has unsuspected limits and can produce altered states of awareness where information, perspective, humour, and the drive to create can be harvested.

But what do we mean by meditiation? It has nothing to do with the popular concept of thinking about something. When a person meditates, the normal process is to attempt to banish thought by lowering the level of internal and external noise and awaken physical or psychological sensations or observations every moment. The subject feels himself filled and emptied in ever larger waves, and little by little, becomes increasingly able to remain in what those of us who practice know as the "fertile vacuum" for longer periods of time. According to a study by the Central Hospital of Massachussetts, a lot can happen in this state, such as increasing cerebral cortex density as though it were being rejuvenated. This is the area of the brain responsible for decision-making, attention and memory.

It's no accident that great meditators need only two or three hours' sleep a night. As shown by delta waves on electro-encephalographs taken during practices, meditators experience express rest with deep sleep and wakefulness. Non-directed and illuminating thoughts that create greater perspective and clarity can also spontaneously emerge from this vacuum.

In conclusion, if you want your physical and psychological health to improve and to open a wider horizon on your life, a better and greater perspective for creativity as well as finding solutions for what arises, practice some form of meditation for a few minutes each day. Empty your mind. The mind, seen as a vessel, needs to be emptied from time to time to make room for new, important things.

07
Innovative Potential. Second Factor: Technological Profile

1. Perception and Technology

Thanks to new technologies it is possible to deploy new business models that would simply have no technical viability if technology were absent. Technology also occupies an essential place in the gestation of the most breakthrough kinds of innovations in the market. For this reason, the relationship between a company's employees and these tools has become a high-impact element in competitive intelligence. This positions the technological profile as the second factor in this dimension, a phenomenon that can be monitored through self-efficacy.

The term self-efficacy was developed by Bandura (1977), in the context of Social Learning Theory where it continues to occupy an important position. It has now expanded to take up centre stage in areas such as health, sports, academia, vocational and organizational decision-making. Bandura defines self-efficacy as "the judgement of every individual concerning his/her abilities on the basis of which he/she will organize and perform his/her actions such that they allow him/her to achieve the desired outcome". The concept makes no reference to the resources available, only to the opinion that the subject holds onto what can be done with them.

Self-efficacy must be differentiated from self-concept, a term that has frequently been misunderstood as a synonym.

Self-concept is our general perception of ourselves, while self-efficacy reflects our opinion about our ability to perform specific actions. An example of the self-concept could be, "I am a great sportsman," while self-efficacy would be expressed as, "I can complete a half-marathon in under 90 minutes."

A person with low expectations of their own performance has no reason to suffer from a poor self-concept. This can be clearly seen when applied to tasks that have a low value. For example, should the fact that we never learnt to programme a video or a camera lead us to think that we aren't intelligent? I don't know how to do it, and so far this has not represented any particular burden for me. Likewise, should the CEO of a successful business feel that his self-concept is under threat because he can't handle Microsoft Excel as skilfully as his secretary? I don't think so.

The opposite relationship, however, does exist. If our self-concept is low, we shall probably not have a high opinion of our ability to perform specific tasks. For example, if I don't see myself as a good sportsperson, am I likely to believe that I could win a hundred metre sprint? I wouldn't even enter the race.

Our self-efficacy assessments are a great predictor of our behaviour. In general, we avoid committing ourselves to undertaking actions that we don't think are within our area of expertise. Our self-efficacy also influences our expectations of achieving goals, which has an effect on our motivation to achieve them, the amount of effort we expend and the time we are prepared to invest in tackling the obstacles that come our way. Indira Gandhi used to warn that, "people who don't think they are capable of doing something will never do it, even though they actually could".

Our self-efficacy also affects the thoughts and emotions associated with an action, before, during and afterwards. This means that it explains to a considerable extent our attitudes and behaviours in such matters as battling disease, making academic choices or facilitating professional careers, but it is also directly related to happiness and quality of life. In the world of sport, it has led to a situation in which physical training is no longer enough. When preparing winners, the trainers of the sporting elite must also train the mind. The rivals of Rafa Nadal, the legendary champion of the French Open, attribute his superiority on the court to his mental strength. After being badly beaten in Paris, David Ferrer admitted to the press that "he has the best mentality I've ever seen. He has everything."

Can this be extrapolated to the field of work? Of course it can. The organizations that aspire to lead in the marketplace must ensure that their teams possess winning mentalities. A word of advice from Rafa Nadal could be of great value to them, "You can never overcome your doubts, you always have to live with them. What you can do is give your best every day and work to make things better." This is the mentality that these companies must look for and encourage.

How is this done? The first step is to understand how our self-efficacy takes shape. According to Bandura's research, there exist four elements upon which self-efficacy develops: experiences of domination, vicarious experiences, degrees of activation and social persuasion.

Experiences of domination are past experiences of success or failure in the execution of the same action and other similar ones. Success results in positive feedback, but so does failure. What this means is that the greater the number of successes we have under our belts, the greater our sense of self-efficacy and vice versa.

Suppose we are really good at a particular sport, so good that we almost always win. Consider the Real Madrid players, for example. What do they expect to happen in the next match? It's a done deal! So how is their ability to deal with the opposition? They are bursting with confidence and in fact, if they don't become overconfident, they may achieve another victory.

When we compare ourselves with others, their abilities and results, this also feeds our perception of ourselves. This gives rise to the second source of expectations, vicarious experiences, from comparisons or second hand. If we always beat the others, always run faster, always score more goals, we will surely end up thinking that we are particularly good in this field.

It's interesting to see the relationship between domination experiences and vicarious experiences. They can complement and buttress each other, but they can also cancel each other out. Let's take a look at that, based on an example. Suppose that although I am quite good at giving presentations in public, so is the rest of the team. Will I feel that I am *especially* good? And what if I'm the only one who is outstanding? In the second case my sense of self-efficacy will surely be greater.

The following exercise will help us to gain insight into this relationship. The first battery represent whether we are particularly good at a task with a +, and with a – if we are not so good. The second covers the skills of our team at this same task. We give them a + if they are good, and a – if not. What is our feeling of self-efficacy going to be in each case?

Figure 7.1 Self-Efficacy Exercise

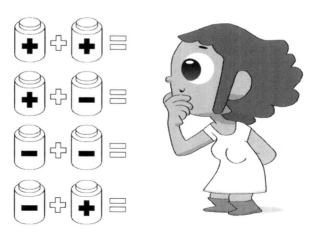

In the first case the vicarious experience might reduce the feeling of self-efficacy gained by the domination experiences, while in the second, by contrast, it will strengthen it. In the third situation, our feeling of self-efficacy will be low because of past experiences, but our knowledge that it is the same for the others will probably mean that it is not excessively low. Let's assume that the task is relatively difficult, and that this is normal. In the final case, this is a job that we find particularly tough, but the others don't seem to find it so, and this is bound to generate a negative perception of self-efficacy which will lead us to avoid the task, and if we can't, we'll end up thinking we aren't able to perform it.

The third source of self-efficacy expectations is our level of physiological and emotional activation (how excited or nervous we become). A high activation level could condition our judgements positively or negatively. It will depend on our mental and emotional states. We all have direct experiences of this. This occurs when, for example, you are well prepared for an exam, but your nerves let you down. Or maybe you prepare so well that you begin to doubt yourself, and in the end you're unable to give your best. Something clouds your mind. I feel certain that it has happened to all of us at least once, when we find ourselves devastated by fear.

And yet, when we feel sure and confident, we are able to make use of our total potential. When the level of excitation is just right and positive, we have a catalyst that can help us give our all. We manage to draw on everything in the conscious and unconscious mind, both objective and subjective, without quite understanding how we succeed.

The final source is social persuasion, the element that reflects the push others can give us to achieve a goal or overcome an obstacle. A motivational speech is an obvious example. This is a much-used tool in the world of sport. How many films have we seen in which, after the trainer has made his pitch, the protagonist becomes convinced of his own superiority, and in the face of all the odds, wins. It's a classic strategy.

Its application and effectiveness are found in all fields – law, politics, war, whatever. Here are some examples from the world of film to show you what I mean. Ed Harris in *Apollo 13* declared, "Failure is not an option." In *Pirates of the Caribbean,* Keira Knightley warned, "and they will know what we can do". Brad Pitt in *Troy* harangued his army with the words, "Let no man forget how menacing we are! We are lions!" And coming back to our everyday lives, who can forget Barack Obama's explosive "Yes we can!"?

How is self-efficacy to be managed? The first step is to clarify the objective. How far do we want to go? Should a good leader convince his team that he is outstanding at everything? Of course not. The objective of self-efficacy must be realistic. Nothing is gained by generating false hopes about what you are and what you can become. The management style you adopt should help each individual understand their abilities and strengths, and also their limitations and weaknesses. It should support their work and boost its potential. Self-efficacy from a false foundation will not only lead to negative experiences and frustration, but will become increasingly unsustainable over time.

On the matter of tools, the answer lies in the sources of the expectations. It might be advisable to fall back on generating positive experiences by allocating tasks that are easy to accomplish. The use of collective comparisons could be very useful. Additionally, support for achieving high activation plus a motivational talk can be a great help, especially when what is needed is a push with a short-term action. But first and foremost, it is essential to establish a sound internal dialogue that favours feelings of self-efficacy.

This, then, is the time to focus attention on technological self-efficacy. This factor includes the opinion we have about our own ability to handle these tools. It makes no reference to our actual resources, only to our opinion and the perception we have of what we can do with our resources.

Following Bandura's research, this perception is formed as a result of a complex process during which a number of factors take effect. It depends on our prior knowledge and preparation, but also on the experiences we've undergone. Also important are the comparisons we make between ourselves and others and the emotions that generates within us.

Technological self-efficacy conditions our relationship with technology and what we do or fail to do with it. If our self-efficacy is low, it is unlikely that we will make efforts to innovate by using it. What for? Our time is better employed doing something else.

A great deal has been said about gender differences in this field. Do they really exist? Do we behave in the same way when it comes to using technology? Many researchers suggest that women have greater resistance to technology than men and there is no shortage of studies that have shown that if the background conditions are the same (knowledge, training and experience), women usually see themselves as less competent than men in this field. By way of example, we could quote the research work undertaken by the Michelle R. Clayman Institute (2008) at Stanford University. This showed that women tend to generate greater anxiety regarding the use of technology, and underestimate their own abilities compared with those of men. However, subsequent evidence revealed that their *actual* skills were at the same level, and that there was *no real difference*.

Are there any consequences that arise from such a false perception? There certainly are. If we go to one extreme, these women are more likely to suffer from technophobia (a fear or, or aversion to, technology), a syndrome that generates rejection and also hostility, impatience and fatigue. This is an irrational and disproportionate reaction. And at the other extreme, the everyday picture leads many women to feel less attracted to technical university courses, and hence, less likely to make a career in those fields. What would be the final consequence? I think we are all well aware of this: their absence from the technology professions.

Of special interest are studies that have analysed the development of this perception over time. Research has shown that in the initial stages of education, both sexes have similar technology self-efficacy expectations. But as education proceeds, the digital breach begins to make itself felt. (Wigfield, Eccles and Pintrich, 1996). Why? As a result of what?

Many people think this is an isolated fact, and that the differences grow in the area of technology alone, but they are wrong. It is a very common phenomenon with regard to almost all technical or scientific subjects. However, this is not the end of the problem; this is just the tip of the iceberg. A number of generalised self-efficacy studies have now shown that women generally feel less skilled than men (Scholz, Gutierrez-Doña, Sud and Schwarzer, 2002).

What lies behind these differences? Why do women feel less competent? Is it a stereotype? Indeed, stereotypes certainly exist and they do carry a large part of the responsibility. Even so, we should widen our view of the genesis of the problem. A number of studies show that high expectations are also involved in female assessment and self-judgements (Hackett, 1995).

This is not to suggest that such stereotypes should not be monitored or corrected. They exist and they are not doing anyone any good. What emerges is the need for a new focus, one capable of generating a change in external conditioning factors as well as within the women themselves, whereby in the new paradigm, they assume the roles that are appropriate for them in which their innovative potential is not wasted.

2. Innova 3DX for the Technological Profile

Technical self-efficacy is normally responsible for between 5 – 15 per cent of our innovative behaviour. In some companies it may be greater, in some less, due to factors such as age, training or work experience. Nevertheless, in all cases it is a crucial element when it comes to being a leader in digital innovation.

Gender-based analysis has yielded the most surprise. In my research, the first measurement undertaken on a 500-point scale showed that men and women achieved exactly the same score of 322. Nearly 300 subjects were used. Is this pure coincidence or a sign that both men and women are actually much closer in their self-efficacy perception as regards technology?

In the rest of the measurements women generally turned out to possess less self-efficacy than men, but the differences were relatively small, which suggests that we are witnessing a paradigm shift in which women will soon adopt the roles appropriate to them in the digital world.

During the period when this transformation is in progress, it will be essential to implement mechanisms that ensure women's positive perception of the use of technologies in order not to waste their creative potential.

Figure 7.2 Technological Profile Test

Instructions: score your opinion on each statement from 0 – 10, with 0 being the lowest score and 10 the highest. You may use decimals if you wish.

1.	The manual is usually all you need to learn a new ICT programme.	_ _ , _
2.	I find it easy to use the internet.	_ _ , _
3.	I have no problem handling new apps.	_ _ , _

4.	I like incorporating new technologies into my work.	— —, —
5.	I like trying out new apps.	— —, —
Average score		— —, —

Result: from 0 – 3.5 (inclusive) very low, from 3.5 – 5 (inclusive) low, from 5 – 6.5 (inclusive) adequate, from 6.5 – 10 (inclusive) very high.

Are you among the "technological adoption leaders", the profile defining those who lead in incorporating new technologies? Or do you prefer to take them on as a "second wave user"? If you want to be a leader you will have to make sure that your self-efficacy is well aligned with the new paradigm.

3. Insight Management and Technological Profile

Creative people used to have moments of inspiration or equally frequently, would find their muses absent as they contemplated a blank page or canvas. Today the format is different; it transcends the traditional physical limits (the size of the canvas or the page, the material to be sculpted, etc.). Thanks to technological advances the physical ground on which work is done is now almost infinite. The materials, too, have changed, as has the way in which the relationship with the medium develops. One could use crayons, paintbrushes and chisels, and express their emotion against the canvas, with genius sometimes appearing in the mode of expression itself. We recognize Van Gogh's brushstrokes or those in action painting as pure, energetic creative expression.

Today an infinity of possibilities opens up beyond our senses. You can paint in the air, without a brush, and technology will record it. You can speak or hum into a microphone and the sheet music will be written for you.

Images take on reality using material textures and different formats, executed thousands of miles away. We live in a world of unheard-of possibilities. Growing up in this culture and learning how to seize it and enjoy it, is a must.

Every company has its own trademark, culture, usages and customs – that either reach out and embrace you and provide security, or stifle you, and suffocate your creativity. It all depends. If fear of change and difference sets like concrete around your feet, you'll never be able to fly towards your dreams. If the company and the people in it ally themselves with life and with the movement of the people who form part of it, they can be witnesses, and support or raise you up, give you wings.

Some people – most in fact – believe that they are not creative because they aren't "naturally" so. They aren't the children whose creative talent was discovered when they were very young or those who studied Humanities at university. But we should not be confused, because creativity travels within us all; it needs no artistic or technical training, although to be honest, if you want good results it's advisable to seek training in both. Nonetheless, those who have natural talent must learn some forms of technological expression. Everybody – from fashion designers, sculptors, advertisers and painters to engineers, accountants, cooks or gardeners – sooner or later move through both zones: creativity and technology. When creativity and technology travel hand-in-hand, they visit new and exciting professional worlds, such as online and offline educational games, simulators, home amusement arcades, remote surgery, vertical gardens and creative culinary technology (using nitrogen, etc.). In all of the above, the focus seems to be on technology, but actually it is on the person and that person's humanity, reproduced technologically.

If the creative agents change, then so do the recipients, as it is certain that they will interact in such a way as to become, in their turn, the communicators. An elite trained in new forms of expression is of little value if there is no witness capable of appreciating them, using them and enjoying them. Again, the receiver has changed at the speed of the radio wave. While many of my generation complained when we had to adapt to the change from Logo to Basic, or from the Spectrum 48K to the Amstrad 127K, it doesn't happen now, and our children at the age of 18 months move images around on a touch screen in the most natural ways possible, puzzled that magazines don't work the same way. Many of their grandparents, our own parents, have also adapted and opened up to new technology and the new horizons the internet provides, not just for news, banking or travel, but also for social networks, looking not only for entertainment, but also a way to find love again.

When it comes to the subject of creativity, everything is possible. When it looked as though artistic forms had been used to the limit, computers appeared and showed us that you could defy gravity and spatial preconceptions and build buildings upside-down, like the Casa de Kathmandu in Majorca. In the same way, a timeline can be reinterpreted so that creation is visualised in real time, with a stroke or step-by-step, or even backward and forward

It's all very technological and *also* very humane. Staying with the network, with technology, this is fundamental and crucial for understanding media, tools and possibilities, but don't take your eye off reality and forget what food tastes like, or what someone else's skin feels like, or the actual scent of flowers. If you become completely submerged in technology, you might end up like in the film *The Matrix,* asleep, believing in a reality that only pretends to be true, disconnected from the real one … happy or deceived? Without awareness we live in ignorance.

When such a level of technological immersion is on offer, how can we cling to reality while living a virtual existence? Easy: by not breaking the connection with life and by disconnecting from technology from time to time. Don't scorn your senses and don't over-protect yourself from the cold, from aromas, from flavours or from love. Experiment with textures. Feel them and look at them and then imagine. Live and then invoke, but above all, live – it's the only way to stay in the here and now, connected to reality.

The temptation to set aside reality in exchange for a virtual experience is always there. If you saw the film "The Big Blue", you recall that moving scene of the diver who enjoys the withdrawn apnoea of the silent ocean more than contact with humans. At last, on one of his dives, drunk with the feeling of his other world, he decides to let go of the descent line and refuse to return to the world of the breathing. It is a beautiful image, certainly, although tragic, because he dies from lack of oxygen.

You should alternate between creativity and pragmatism, between intangible technology and the tangible. Move, dare to travel in one direction or another. Explore, live, dream and turn your dreams into reality. Create, enjoy, relate with technology, but never cease to care for your body, look after yourself, hone your physical presence, your affections, etc. If you don't, sooner or later you will begin to pay for it and will end up like the diver.

Changing the subject, if what is tangible, real, or even seems to be real, is what reminds you that you're here, then what lies within the vacuum is what really allows you to create and discover. If you study a stippled wall you will see many shapes that remind you of something, connections that the brain makes, evoking something. First, allow yourself to sink into the vacuum, then relax and allow the parts to come together within your vision, and suddenly there it appears, the famous three-dimensional image, the stereogram, that at first you can't make out, and then, when you relax, you can. The same thing happens with creativity. Let yourself go, give your energy permission to move, don't constrict yourself. Have a good time, laugh, move, scream if you feel like it, jump and contort your body, dance. Give free rein to your creative process, not just the mental side, but the physical side, too. When the sluice gate opens, water sweeps away all the obstacles and brings messages from afar, which are not only different but also enriching and illuminating.

If self-efficacy depends on a person's self-concept, on whether he feels capable or not, as well as on the effectiveness with which they believe it, discarding prejudices means that you are freeing yourself from the shackles that stop you from travelling. A famous photographer once told me her rather nice version of the situation: she was a psychologist by qualification, but a photographer by profession, yet she had never managed to learn how to program a video recorder, despite how often her husband and son explained it to her, because according to her, "I shall never be able to understand technology."

One day she overheard a work colleague explaining the range of opportunities that opened up if you changed the reflex camera for a digital camera. She set aside her prejudices, bought a digital camera and the very next day she was operating it – to the amazement of all, including her husband, an engineer who had always dealt with the technological stuff because she thought herself "incapable". Motivation was, of course, crucial, but before that, it was essential for her to set aside her prejudice in thinking she wasn't capable. This example, illustrates the most common gender issue but finally, you have to allow yourself to be what you want to for once, rather than what you've been taught to be. Everything's OK as long as it's decided freely, either on an individual basis or as a partnership.

In just the same way that she underwent this experience with technology, there are some people and companies associated with the world of photography in particular, or technology in general, who were, or still are, resistant, and have perished, or will perish. An excellent example is the at the time all-powerful and universal Kodak, now on the brink of disappearance despite their resistance, because they weren't prepared to cease clinging to what they possessed; they were unwilling to close in time and start something new other than their self-identification with a product, a technique, etc. Transitions from the summit to collapse that used to take from 3 to 5 years now happen in 6 to 12 months. Nowadays, if you want to survive, you simply have to reinvent yourself every now and again.

As we shall explore in-depth in other sections, it is very important to work on yourself and develop an internal frame of reference, beyond self-esteem based on successes and being better than others. If you're still one of those people who needs to compete in order to grow, seek out your enemies to observe them and motivate yourself to grow. As Sinatra said, in the end there is no better way than "my way".

I am fascinated by the story of elite athletes, like Michael Jordan, the basketball player who in his time was so much better than the other players that he stopped competing against them and invented imaginary enemies to stretch himself. This was brought to the cinema in a film that blended animation with real people ("Space Jam"). A word of warning: it's tough for a team to play with a star. And another tip, if in a competition I see that I'm no good at something that everybody else is good at, the best thing I can do is to delegate, subcontract and devote my energy to something I can do.

On the road to self-efficacy, emptying yourself means travelling light, with no heavy burdens in your backpack. If you're completely full up, if you think that nothing can take you by surprise, you will find it very difficult to be receptive and pay attention so that you can see reality as it actually is – and you'll simply be unable to take anything on board. People like this are weighed down, asleep, just like the people who thought they knew everything and had to experience bankruptcy so they could understand that even a large, successful business could crash. In other words, if you want to stay alive and keep learning, start from scratch, every day. Take a look at the sky to see what colour it is, sense how the water tastes, what the markets are doing and how your partner is. If you never stop looking, without judging, you'll appreciate the changes around you that allow you to learn, develop, adapt and be successful.

"He who does not grow will die", said Gladstone, the prime minister of Britain during the height of 19th century imperialism, following Darwin's rationale. But now we are forced to add another turn of the screw and remember that, "he who fails to shrink, does not grow, and hence, dies". You need humility to survive and grow professionally and personally. People who refuse to shrink in order to survive and instead grow, will not survive. As we learn from Lewis Carroll in "Alice's Adventures in Wonderland," if you want to get through the door, you must grow or shrink as needed. I encourage you to drink in some wit to do that.

08
Innovative Potential. Third Factor: the Psychological Profile (I)

1. Personality and Translation of Reality (I)

Our innovative potential is conditioned by four personality traits: self-esteem, optimism, locus of control and orientation towards learning. All play a part in the translation of individual reality conditioning our behaviour. They effect the effort we dedicate to a job and our expectations of successfully completing it, and also on the thinking and emotions that go along with it, before, during and afterwards. In the field of work they have an effect on our degree of commitment, motivation and productivity. Therefore let's start with a few lines about the personality.

The etymological roots of the word are not clear, but it is assumed to derive from a Greek word *prosopon,* the mask used by the actors in the ancient Greek theatre. Since that time, the meaning has developed considerably until now it is used to define the concept that best reflects the inner self, representing a pattern of cognitive, affective and behavioural traits that remain stable over time, affecting all aspects of behaviour.

In light of the scope and power of its influence, the personality has overstepped the frontiers of psychology and found a home in the field of business management, where it's used to provide new techniques and tools for boosting motivation and productivity. Since innovation is essentially a human process, the research and literature that have risen around personality haven't drifted far from that perception.

1.1. Self-Esteem

According to the dictionary, the verb "to esteem", means "to appreciate, to put a price on, to value something". Other definitions include "to judge, to believe". Self-esteem is thus the value that we put on ourselves. It is not something that reflects what others think of us; it is the outcome of our own measuring.

It is helpful when trying to grasp its meaning to compare it with 'self-concept', an element that clearly has a different meaning, although often used as a synonym. A self-concept is the cognitive structure that reflects who you are. It includes how you see yourself. By contrast, self-esteem shows the judgement you pass on yourself.

It's also important not to confuse self-esteem with narcissism, which would be a serious mistake. Narcissism means self-admiration to the level of pathology, or excessive love for oneself. Indeed, not only are they not synonymous, they are frequently opposites. A high level of narcissism is almost always associated with low self-esteem. Narcissism is a defence mechanism. In its acute stage it may be diagnosed as a mental disturbance: narcissistic personality disturbance (American Psychiatric Association, 1994).

Self-esteem affects every minute of your existence. This means that healthy self-esteem is essential for your life processes to operate on a normal footing. It functions like your immune system, providing strength and resistance. In fact, when your self-esteem level is low, your resistance to the adversities of life is also low.

Good self-esteem provides fortitude, energy and motivation. People with high self-esteem are more ambitious in all aspects of life, and have a greater likelihood of success. They seek to learn from vital experiences and are prepared to confront challenges. They appear resistant to collapse because they are happier. Indeed, people with healthy self-esteem are normally more optimistic and have a better sense of humour. Interestingly, they also seem to be more attractive than others.

By contrast, a low level of self-esteem is a well-known cause of physiological and psychological disturbance. Such subjects feel weaker and are more negative about their ability to confront their own challenges. For this reason they seek security and avoid uncertainty. They are also more vulnerable and find it hard to deal with everyday life problems. They are less happy, less attractive and less successful, which makes for a negative spiral that feeds back on itself and grows.

Abraham Maslow, the well-known American psychologist, summed it up very neatly, "satisfying the need for self-esteem leads to a feeling of self-confidence, worth, strength, capability and sufficiency, of being useful and necessary in the world". As Eleanor Roosevelt, former US First Lady, put it, "Nobody is allowed to make you feel smaller without your consent."

How does it come about? Why is it that some people have high self-esteem and others do not? How does it evolve over time? Can you boost your own self-esteem? How should you manage the teams' self-esteem? Where do you start?

Children come into this world with psychological features established by their genes. But factors such as experience, social identity and the environment soon affect them. Although these are not the only factors, they are the most important, and require special attention.

Self-esteem is a concept largely built on images fed by past experiences. Especially significant are childhood experiences. A child who has had experiences that generated positive responses and reactions will tend to develop better self-esteem. Of course, we all have negative and positive experiences. Self-esteem is not the product of one or even a few experiences: it is the result of total life experience.

Self-esteem is also a feature of individual personality that is very closely associated with social identity. A person who identifies with a group will take on most of its characteristics as part of their own identity. Sporting groups, for example, show this very clearly. They take on the good, but also the bad, which is why such identification processes need to be monitored.

In the workplace the climate, culture and style of leadership and management also affect self-esteem. A "bad" leader – one who not only fails to stimulate self-esteem but seems determined to crush it – cannot expect positive results, at least as far as innovation is concerned. His team will not be motivated and will make no efforts. A good leader doesn't forget how important it is and how it must be cultivated, or at least not damaged. The first thing that a good leader does is cultivate their own self-esteem.

It goes without saying that physical appearance and intellectual capacity may also affect it, but they are not determining features. What is a determining feature is the attitude with which they are integrated.

Self-esteem is an element that can and should be taught. It is something that must be cultivated. Sound self-esteem is something only you, yourself, can generate. People committed to nurturing it will succeed in raising it. This means that step one is to accept yourself as you are, with your weaknesses and limitations, and then to live with an awareness of what the future might hold.

I would like to relay something from my own personal experience. I was fortunate to meet some extraordinary professionals – managers possessing natural management styles that made me want to be under their tutelage and follow their lead, go where they went. Fortunately at the same time,

I came across others whose self-esteem was quite eroded. I say fortunately, because I learnt a great deal from them. They taught me lessons I shall never forget (or repeat), and I am grateful to them.

1.2. Optimism

The dictionary defines this as, "the propensity for seeing and judging things in the most favourable light". There are positive and negative events in every life. What makes optimists different is the way they explain their life experiences, because they choose to see the positive side of things, even when they are actually negative. They display an enthusiasm for life and what it brings, which makes them happier people. Because of that, it looks as though life is smiling on them.

Optimism affects your health (physical and mental), social sphere (family, love, friendships), and, of course, educational and work lives.

Optimism protects your health. Faced with uncertainty, optimists have positive expectations that all will turn out for the best (Scheier and Carver, 1985). This means that they are less exposed to stress and the likelihood that they will suffer from it is reduced. But there's more. Studies were designed and undertaken to predict illness in healthy people, and empirical research showed that optimism is associated with fewer cardiovascular diseases, among others (Kubzanski *et al.*, 2001). Similarly, people already suffering from an illness were shown to suffer fewer complications (Helgeson y Fritz, 1999). In short, optimists enjoy better health and live longer than their fellows (Carver, Scheier y Segerstrom, 2010). No better medicine exists to protect your health. And it's free.

Optimism is very easy to notice and the reaction to it is almost always contagious. An optimist floods their life space with positive thinking and stimulates those around them. A pessimist, by contrast, carries thoughts of failure and doubtlessly perceives and probably replicates them in their vicinity.

Optimism boosts energy, so that optimists are normally more persistent, particularly in the face of adversity. Faced with a problem, an optimist focuses on seeking solutions and sees each failure as an opportunity to learn something. There exists a positive relationship between optimism and self-efficacy. What all this means is that optimism is a mental attitude found in successful persons in all walks of life. Pessimists, on the other hand, tend to build elements of personal blame into their explanations, especially when negative events take place. Phrases like, "Just my luck," and "it could only happen to me" are very common in their personal discourse and can lead to even more pessimism and more sapped energy. When a failure occurs, pessimists concentrate on the mistake and seek what to blame instead of learning from the experience. In brief, pessimism filters reality, and prevents you from bringing all available resources into play. And this, naturally enough, will be seen in your academic and professional output.

Everybody possesses natural optimism, usually more easily observable in childhood. Some people seem to contain a strong predisposition for humour and happiness, while others lean more towards unease and irritability. This means that change is possible, but it will call for lots of personal effort.

2. Innova 3DX for the Psychological Profile (I)

Self-esteem and optimism have an obvious effect on your behaviour as innovators. They are a part of your thinking, the way you are: if the culture is innovative, if you feel at home in the company, if you're lucky enough to have a great leader as a boss, if you're a creative individual, if you have good technological self-efficacy … but if you feel pessimistic or perceive yourself to have low value, will you try to innovate?

It's possible that you might and that you will but you'll never give it your all. You won't feel like it, won't get it together. Your own personal blockages will prevent you.

In other words, these two personality traits can operate as powerful catalysts or turn into obstacles, preventing you from making use of all your potential as though your creative impulse were paralysed. This means that you have to take on new management models that consider human capital from this new perspective. It may not be easy, but it is essential if the innovation machine is to operate at full throttle.

Figure 8.1 Self-Esteem and Optimism Test

Instructions: score your opinion on each statement from 0 – 10, with 0 being the lowest score and 10 the highest. You may use decimals if you wish.

Self- esteem (Questions designed on the basis of the Rosenberg scale, 1965.)		
1.	I feel comfortable with myself.	__ __ , __
2.	I know my strengths.	__ __ , __
3.	I like to take my own decisions.	__ __ , __
4.	I am a capable person.	__ __ , __
5.	I like being the way I am.	__ __ , __
Average score		__ __ , __
Optimism (Questions designed on the basis of the Scheier, et al., scale, 1994.)		
1.	I look on the bright side of life.	__ __ , __
2.	I seldom feel sad.	__ __ , __
3.	Sometimes I just know things will turn out all right.	__ __ , __
4.	I see the future with enthusiasm.	__ __ , __
5.	I usually feel happy.	__ __ , __
Average score		__ __ , __

Result: from 0 – 3.5 (inclusive) very low, from 3.5 – 5 (inclusive) low, from 5 – 6.5 (inclusive) adequate, from 6.5 – 10 (inclusive) very high.

Figure 8.2 Psychological Profile Quadrant (I)

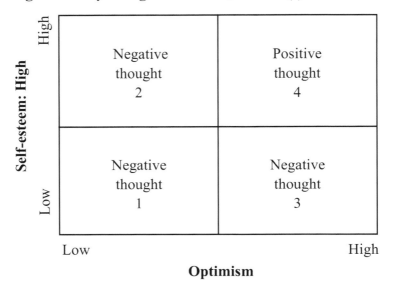

In the fourth quadrant you can find those who practice "positive thinking". These are people who have high self-esteem and see the future with optimism. This is the mental attitude found among people who are successful.

In comparison, in the other quadrants, we find people who devote their time to looking for culprits, for who to blame and even courting problems. These are the people who practice "negative thinking".

The power of both thought patterns is enormous, but only the first is more profitable. The best choice is obvious.

3. Insight Management, Self-Esteem and Optimism

3.1. Self-Esteem

Many years ago I was told a story about an eagle's egg which had accidentally fallen into a hen's nest. When the eagle hatched it tried to imitate its "siblings" in the way they walked, because it was the last and did not want to attract attention, copying them in everything, trying hard to do it well, but the fact is that it was a bit slow on the uptake and the others laughed at it. The time passed, and one day it raised its eyes to the heavens and saw a real eagle, majestically floating on the air high in the sky, demonstrating all its power and wonderful presence. The chick really wanted to fly, but it had had no lessons, and when it tried it fell clumsily to the earth, much to the amusement of its siblings who mocked it, telling it that it would never fly. And the poor eagle believed them, stopped trying and died like a queer and clumsy chicken.

It's important to tackle self-esteem from the point of view of identity: in a world where strenuous efforts are made to shape people from a very early age, people end up believing what they are told they are, instead of spreading their wings and deploying their maximum potential in the direction that draws them. Everybody knows that child prodigies are often somewhat socially inept, even seriously neurotic, because of the difficulty of battling with a programming machine that attacks us on all fronts: school, parental upbringing, society, other children and even themselves, etc.

We should allow no-one to force us away from our identity, or to interfere with it. Have the confidence to spread your wings and fly, or swim, crawl, whatever suits you best, find your own speciality. And do the same with your children and staff. Support, encourage, stimulate, motivate and help, and observe the evidence.

If self-esteem is built around others' expectations and social success, what lies within will remain imprisoned, inhibited and dependent on external prompts yet having limited contact with what's inside. Where there is initial success, self-esteem remains falsely suspended from a brilliant self-image and then it becomes very difficult to reconcile that image in times of failure. But you should remember that failure comes to all sooner or later (at work, with a partner, boss, wife, children, friends, etc.). Narcissism and depression are in reality both sides of the same coin, and have little to do with healthy self-esteem.

Crises create an opportunity for reviewing past deficiencies that during times of abundance went unnoticed. Every day I meet more employees with brilliant CVs who come to me with serious self-esteem problems because no one is hiring them now, and their image, or market or exchange value simply foundered or disappeared, leaving price, value and self-esteem all confused.

The value and esteem in which something or someone is held should never be confused with exchange value. This subject is as old as the discussions between Plato and Aristotle, but in our consumer society we've lost sight of the frame of reference that shows what things and people are worth in our desperate efforts to anchor ourselves to a fantasy world of what the market once said they were worth.

The situation is quite obvious when you talk about real estate, but what happens when the crisis reaches people? Managers whose narcissism was for years flattered by high salaries and social recognition suddenly found themselves out of work with not so much as a job interview for two years. Their self-esteem crumbled with the passage of days, weeks and months. They spiralled down into an abyss that was noticed by possible employers who obviously did not give them a chance. They had never developed an internal frame of reference for perceiving their true worth, assuming their value was a function of the image they reflected back on themselves, and they're still doing this today. This is a mistake.

Self-esteem must always be located within the intrinsic value of being. Just by virtue of the fact that I exist means that I deserve to be loved by others and by myself. It doesn't depend on the fact that I earn x amount, or that I have so many people under me. That is all circumstantial. Sometimes it happens, sometimes it doesn't, but the value of a person continues the same. In any case, the narcissism of the beginning is as damaging as the subsequent depression. They are false perceptions of reality and they destroy relationships because they are based on assumptions of superiority or inferiority.

It is very important not to lose sight of the real value of things. Thus, when you are very much in demand, you should always be aware of the fact that you are no more, and no less than other people and workers. Knowing this will circumvent rampant narcissism or destructive depression, and allow you to carry on humbly working towards the right place. If you don't, then life, like a Zen master, will come with its hard stick and show you as many times as it is necessary that your value is immense and has nothing to do with whom you believe you are, because this is different; it's real, and it's not an exchange value.

I want to make special mention of the loss of self-esteem that's caused by workplace ambush, or mobbing. I don't intend to explore this in-depth, but just want to mention that everybody whose self-esteem is based on images handed out by their boss is a potential victim. People who aspire to external recognition in order to love themselves may find themselves with a sick boss (sick through envy, demands, avarice, complexes, etc.) for whom nothing is ever enough, and from there on, the catch and the angler are one and the same. If you want to stay away from this one, then don't take the bait. Just do your work as honestly as you can and clearly communicate what you can and can't do. It will cost you to put up with your boss's fears, but it will save your physical and mental health.

By contrast, I want to point out that in the mobbing war, both players are usually aggressors and victims, despite all appearances. The movement may start from above with a dreadful boss who is tormented with envy, gives no recognition, steals ideas and endlessly demands more, etc. He is someone who not only has no talent, he also has no self-esteem, because if he did, he would know how to support his team, and how to stand like a tree with majestic branches on which bloom beautiful flowers. If this doesn't happen, sooner or later envy and suspicion appear and result in aggression that will soon enough become obvious to both sides.

There tend to be two types of response: one is aggressive, where you confront the boss and threaten him while the other is submissive, where you allow yourself to be humiliated in the hope of receiving approval that never comes. In either case, the conflict that fails to be resolved with the passage of time will serve to buttress feelings of resentment. This doesn't improve the atmosphere. It thins it still further, turning it into a spiral of more or less well-concealed aggression. And that has tragic results for the victim, whose physical and psychological scars may last for years – as they will for the bully or wielder of power, who as a person, also possesses fissures and gaps.

Beyond the subject of self-esteem and how to contain and multiply it in all directions, is the subject of personal power. When I think about somebody's personal power, I first think about where it is rooted. If you have power, but it has no roots, it isn't worth anything. Think of a 150-foot-tall giant redwood with a half inch root. However imposing it may seem, the first gust of wind will bring it down. So if anybody wishes to enjoy their power to the full, apart from being physically well anchored, with corporal exercises and the feeling of weight in their feet, they must remember what and how deep their roots are. Roots are father, mother, grandparents, ancestors, hometown, language, country, race, etc. Everything that defines you and gives you body and presence of the kind you possess. The opposite – denying your origins – is to disagree with them or wish to be something or someone else. Doing that blurs and diffuses the picture and renders it confused, weak and frail. Could you imagine Nelson Mandela pretending to not be black? His power would vanish.

We must drive our lives from our gut and inject passion into all we do , while being confident about it. When you feel that your belly is full and that life proceeds from that space, it means you're centred, you don't need to go anywhere else to be filled, and your value doesn't evolve from comparisons to anyone. You have no need to compete with anything or anyone; you are simply complete, you simply are. Acting from the gut also means being able to digest and contain the sound self-esteem I spoke of earlier. If your self-esteem is well constructed, you don't ever fear loss when you work as part of a team. You can rely on the others as allies in an "enterprise" – in the sense of journey. The opposite is crazy – travelling alone and with no help – not only calls for enormous effort, but greatly reduces your capacity to survive in any walk of life.

Closely associated with this point is the heart. When you possess power it means you can do what you want to do, contribute from an abundant source, leave aside feeling impoverished or wanting. You feel capable of giving – which ensures that prosperity flows towards you, possibly in the form of people whom you wish to reward. Giving and receiving, or receiving and giving. As it says in Buddhism, the Bible and many other places, "give and ye shall receive".

There is no doubt that power would not be power if it were not focused in one direction, with one intention. If you locate existential longings, you should put your power to their service, express your own voice and command for that purpose. If you don't find them, then look for them, rather than dashing about like a maniac in all directions. If you still can't locate them then you must proceed in one direction, exploring, looking, making sure you know when and where the direction changes. The path passes through things as trivial as: What would I like to eat? Where do I want to sit? Where do I want to sleep? Am I thirsty? Listen to your inner voice. Without finding your centre on these questions you cannot start to ask yourself about greater issues.

If you continue to advance your concentration on power, you'll see that the mind makes use of a double perspective: one is analytic, based on Cartesian logic; and the other is intuitive, where vision has another kind of depth, another form of listening based on a multitude of sensory and pseudo-sensory registers that it takes into account.

If you place yourself in the service of your own mission, yield yourself to it and relax, you will flow with life and make good use of your personal power and you will enjoy it.

Writing on these subjects may lead to poor readings, and in that case all I can do is encourage you to always question what you are doing with your power. It often happens that someone who is striving to evolve and grow, to be good or whatever you like to call it, will find that they are polarised at one end of their personality's pendulum and will feel impoverished without swinging to the other extreme where, for example, selfishness might be a virtue in a specific context.

Here I take the liberty to share the story of my great-great-great grandfather, an Urrea like myself. He chose the road of religion and rose rapidly to the rank of the Archbishop of Tarragona, whereupon he set off to battle with "the Turk" in the Mediterranean in the middle of the fifteenth century. Here he ended up turning into what was certainly the first and last pirate archbishop in history, probably because, believing himself to be in possession of the Truth, and duly granting himself appropriate rights, he set out to sack and pillage wherever he could. The Pope himself, who pronounced an anathema on him, was unable to imbue him with a social conscience, and he continued to plunder "archiepiscopally" until it fell to King Alonso V to successfully call him to heel, and duly returned him to his see in Tarragona, where his standard still hangs in the cathedral.

This story, coming from six centuries ago might appear somewhat ancient, but quite to the contrary in fact, it is quite up to date, and needs airing to cast a light on true human nature.

We are all angels and devils, treading life's highways doing good and evil with or without power or awareness. It is very important that you don't start believing in the dress we wear, whether it be that of an archbishop, a politician, a doctor, a teacher, a fighter for equality or a therapist, because without exception, all are angels and devils.

We cannot help being reminded that recovering self-esteem and personal power costs a great deal, and that you must always be on the alert not to lose them. In a battle the lance which is anchored in the ground against the enemy who hurls himself upon it is deadly, because it never withdraws, and can be used again. The lance which is thrown afar may strike or it may not, but we have certainly lost it and its usefulness if we fail to recover it.

You must closely keep watch on who or what you bestow your power to: a work addiction, a potential mate, alcohol, sex or other drugs. It's even possible you'd give it all up to indolence or even the narcissism mentioned earlier. Being aware of your power and self-esteem leaks is as important as, and possibly more important than, the way you win or recapture it

A good boss should be able to exercise his power as an authority in an impeccable manner, with concern for each and every one of those under his control. He should exercise his power without getting in their way and without causing obstructions. The opposite is foolish authoritarianism which is petty, weakening, limiting and which rottens the workplace climate and foments internecine struggles that don't help.

I feel I should end with a word on self-esteem as seen through the gender spectrum. In *Eloísa o la existencia de la mujer* [Eloise or the Existence of Women (1945)], Spanish essayist and philosopher María Zambrano said that men need to create a character so that they can watch themselves live, so that they can get to know themselves, as though through this definition;

meantime women manage to live without definition, live more within themselves, beyond the heart – directly – not needing to invent an alter ego as men do.

Almost 70 years after our beloved and brilliant María, we find ourselves constrained to suggest that things have changed. Many women have unconsciously taken on identifying with aspects of masculinity in order to compete the way men do in the masculine world of work. The pit has been dug, the trap set and the victims caught. Many – too many – professional women have lost contact with the experience of the inner life that Zambrano talks about, and have sacrificed their essential femaleness towards defending their position in a masculine world.

To conclude, this new century will witness transformation one way or another, with people incorporating their polarities (angel/devil, female/male, etc.) to a greater degree. The challenge matters, because moving towards internal and external equilibrium will lead to an evolutionary leap with repercussions on both personal and professional levels, but in order to achieve it we shall have to pay attention, work hard on our personal evolution, always question ourselves, and communicate and listen, either by ourselves or as a group.

3.2. Optimism

In our vain society, selling the 'be an optimist' line may not be the best way to go and might even be counterproductive. The image of vanity implies optimism, but it's painted, so has become sweetened and false. "They hide the bodies under the carpet, take a couple of Valium and put a good face on it, because they're optimists," think the fake survivors with their wooden faces, gritted teeth and stiff upper lips. This is not optimism, this is adaptation, and it lacks grace.

Discussing optimism may even be counterproductive, since to write, speak or lecture about optimism with a view to convincing others may just irritate people who need to first complain, weep and work out their anger. We should be very careful in these times of crisis, when every family lives with tragedy in the form of a pay cut or a lost job, and if not your own, then that of a sibling, parent or child. Treat the subject with special care and tact, with yourself and everybody else.

Therefore let's air out the proverbial room, open the windows and empty the drawers. Let's clean what exhausts us, what's dead, what doesn't contribute. Purge your emotions the way it suits you, with therapy or sport or time with your friends, and do it until you don't need to do it anymore, as often as you please. Then take a look at your circumstances – the cards you have to play in life – and learn to make the most of your luck.

If you insist on staring at what Father Christmas didn't bring you, you'll be a miserable kid your whole life. If you concentrate on what he did bring, you might feel grateful for it and consequently make your own contributions to life, which will undoubtedly be returned again and again in a spiral of positive feedback. Who gives, receives; who waits, despairs.

Adopting a positive attitude to life fills you with a passion to achieve more, always looking at the full part of the glass and working to fill it fuller still. By contrast, always looking as what's missing leaves you even shorter and hence unhappy. The consumer society has a thousand and one twisted ways of leaving us with that feeling of unhappiness, because you can always consume something better, or at least something more expensive. Don't be fooled, happiness has nothing to do with that.

Remember the body commands for good and evil: If you drag on with your head down you'll see neither the landscape nor your next goal. Physiologically your chest will be constricted, your lungs will never fill completely, your back will ache, your stomach will shrink and the sensation of lack of energy and depression will meet to form a desperate feeling. Have a good stretch, look up, head held high, take a deep breath, stick out your chest and get moving towards life with strength, power and courage.

Optimism generates energy since it uses passion as its engine. It is intelligently economical and ecological, since an optimist doesn't waste resources – but finds them within – and loses no energy, in fact, is more likely to generate synergy-type environments where there's give and take, the kind that nourishes on many levels. Think, write and then remember: what are the things that rob me of energy, passion, enthusiasm and strength? If you can, do it, get down to the details and separate out the various levels: physiological, mental, emotional and even spiritual. Although many deny it, spiritual connections are great sources of energy, passion, confidence and optimism. When you've finished your list, don't just toss it into a drawer. Put it up on the refrigerator. Review it every week. Take notice of it – you wrote it yourself!

Many people assume that an in-depth analysis must include diet, habits, company, atmosphere, etc. Remember that what is not added is subtracted. If you want to speed towards your life goals like a rocket, don't waste any strength on the way. In my own case there were years when I felt half-asleep. I had no energy to attack big projects, particularly after eating. Once I did some research I found that I had dietary intolerances, and that gluten was not only causing my intestines to swell, it was also a toxin that forced my digestion into using high levels of energy every day that left me with none for anything else. Giving it the elbow was frustrating, since I enjoy a lot of gluten-rich foods, but when I gave them up, I started to feel much better and more energetic.

I'm not just talking about diet; I'm talking about intolerances, toxins, respect for your body and not endlessly subjecting yourself to tests. If you find you have to give something up, do it with affection and friendship, even allowing yourself the occasional treat if you must. I award myself a pizza or a few biscuits from time to time, which makes my journey less harsh and more sustainable.

Make your own review or list in your own way – it will be very interesting. I assure you that when I reviewed my energy sources and drains I found some surprises, like old connections, ex-partners, friends, even cyber-friends who, far from contributing, took up space, energy and time, generated noise and distracted me, subtracting from what I had available. The review also helped me cast my moorings away from ports where I no longer collected provisions – like circles, spaces, attitudes or customs that no longer nourished me. There is no reason why something that used to work will continue doing so, either professionally or personally.

Make a list that is practical, short, real and reasonable. You don't have to work out an interlocking astral chart for each person with whom you work or operate in some relationship with; you don't need a consultant to *feng shui* your house and you don't have to cast the I Ching. If you're accustomed or comfortable with that and know what you're doing, go ahead, but it really isn't necessary. Using much simpler details like listening carefully and checking whether you eat when you're hungry, drink when you're thirsty, put the light on when the sun has gone down or turn the TV down because it makes too much noise, you'll gain a great deal, maybe enough to grant yourself the energy you need to achieve what you want to.

Changing the subject, bear in mind that all the internal work you do, of whatever kind, will go in the direction of optimism because that is where all of you, including your lighter and darker sides converges. You'll not only discover your self-destructive tendencies, but also very common phenomena such as the "poor little me" fraud.

This attitude, which includes the "poor little me, nothing I do ever comes out right; poor little me, nobody loves me; poor little me, the boss doesn't understand me; poor little me, I didn't have a loving family; poor little me, they never pay me what I deserve" needs to be worked through and cleared out. If not, that voice becomes a real energy drain to your and everybody else's energy. Initially it may seem that this victim mentality gets others to help you, but as time passes, people will start avoiding you, which will feed your idea that you're a victim. Your attitude will drive them away and you'll turn yourself into a self-fulfilling prophecy of a victim.

Working on yourself is hard, but it is extremely fruitful, since it helps you with the cracks in your self-esteem, fears, confidence in life in general and in yourself in particular. It also boosts your optimism and reinforces your sense of belonging to something greater (team, family, community, etc.) which will support you to build and grow.

If you experience problems with belonging and you still feel very much on your own, then be grateful for what you *are* given and the support that you *do* receive. I give thanks every day for many things, just like my grandmother used to do – from meals to services, my children's teachers and the huge network of support I rely on. Suddenly I feel very small – less great, less self-sufficient, less arrogant, less "I can do it myself, I don't need anyone", and also less alone and more accompanied. I feel infinitely grateful for this whole network of people, great and small, who give me the feeling of belonging and who make the life I've chosen possible. My ego shrinks to a healthier, more humble and human size, and I recognize that I need others, which opens my heart to everything and everybody, and makes me want to contribute still more.

No one person could build the pyramids or discover America, but in collaboration with others it could be done. Remember that we all drive and are driven. Hence, humility and gratitude towards others allow you to not only see your own abundance, but to recognize each individual's importance and keep your team duly motivated for new battles.

Before concluding, I want to mention some concepts that go along with optimism: resilience, fluidity, creativity and humour. Resilience is concerned with the faculty possessed by some to take advantage of even extremely adverse circumstances, so that by learning from these situations, they emerge stronger. This quality derives from the desire to never stop learning, which is a characteristic of sages and of the powerful who are not only never destroyed, but the ones who triumph via their persistence.

> "Perceiving what is subtle is illumination, knowing your weakness is strength."
>
> *Tao Te Ching*

How does one become resilient? The *Tao Te Ching* does not tell you to simply put up with things or that you must be stronger; it encourages you to perceive the subtle, to know your own weakness, to make yourself flexible and soft. Remember this in extreme conditions and in crises, in situations where most people are scared and so pull with all their might, harden themselves and expose themselves to death, to breaking apart inside.

> "Unyielding hardness is death's companion. The soft and gentle are life's companions. Forceful armies will not win. Trees unable to bend will ultimately yield to the axe. The strong and stiff will fall. The soft and supple will endure."
>
> *Tao Te Ching*

Flow, flow like water among rocks, seek your way downstream to pour out into the sea. Don't strive to make it back upstream or in a straight line. This is madness and cannot be done. Follow the easy way, always favouring movement. If movement in one direction is blocked, take the other direction. To remove blockages, rely on creativity, go down to the well of emptiness with confidence, because here we all add and take away. You'll be surprised. You'll find that your resources are much greater than you thought.

And lastly, laugh. Laugh until the tears flow, or laugh in secret, but laugh. You'll feel much better for it than when you cling to negative feelings and bad temper. Your body, mind and your spirit and those of everybody around you will thank you for it. If you feel you have no reason to laugh, invent one, laugh at yourself, at the situation, at how grotesque it all is, at what is inevitable, you can even laugh at death if you like. Laughing will help you to fill your lungs with good, fresh air all over again. Your tissues will be nourished, your circulation will flow better and the happiness levels inside and around you will multiply ten-fold.

09
Innovative Potential. Second Factor: Psychological Profile (II)

1. Personality and Reality Translation (II)

1.1. Locus of Control

The term locus (or centre) of control comes from the Latin locus, (plural, *loci*) which is translated as the *place* of control. This concept which represents our perception of the cause-effect relationship between our actions and our environment was developed by Rotter (1966).

The locus of control includes our perception of government and responsibility for the events that surround us. People with an internal locus of control believe that the facts that surround their existence are the result of their own behaviour and actions. On the other hand, those who have an external locus of control believe they are the consequence of chance or others' actions. These are people who believe that success and failure do not depend on personal attitudes or efforts. As you would imagine, most of us are located at neither of those extremes, but we often tend to drift towards one of them.

When we blame a professional failure on our own strength or actions, we position ourselves under the locus of internal control, while when we blame it on the environment, bad luck or the crisis, we are under the external locus. It is likely that both are partly responsible; but what matters is the perception of the person for the reasons behind the failure and their perception of chance.

People who locate it within themselves face up to threats and battle to achieve their dreams. Those who place it outside themselves often become chronic complainers who feel victimised. They are irritated and angry and live with fear and bitterness while their lives pass them by.

It is very human to lean towards the external locus of control because it provides a focus for blame and frees the subject from responsibility. Indeed, on some occasions adopting this position may be a question of survival. Faced with a tough breakup or an unexpected job loss, "It was all my partner's fault, she's a real ****," or "it was all my boss's doing, he's a complete ****," makes things much easier, but as the days pass, you have to start working on the internal aspects. You have to ask yourself questions like: How responsible am I? What can I do so that this doesn't happen again? This is the only way to learn from life experiences and develop through them. If you don't do this, you become another name on the list of victims, harbouring grudges and therefore losing the opportunity to learn.

In the world of work, people with an internal locus of control are usually less isolated, more satisfied with their jobs, more accepting of a change of function and usually experience less stress. These are the people who make greater efforts, set more ambitious goals and usually achieve success. Their profiles have a greater predisposition for leadership and entrepreneurship – highly valued qualities in these times.

By contrast, people with an external locus of control are much less predisposed to expend effort, and instead, reveal lower levels of performance and set much less ambitious goals for themselves. They have a greater predisposition to anxiety, stress and depression. This naturally leads to a lower level of success in their professional careers. They think, "Why should I make the effort? There's no point."

A great deal of research has regarded the locus of control as an element having a direct effect on business success. For example, Gilad (1982), showed that the internal locus of control is related to a state of being that is alert and on the watch for fresh opportunities, with a nose for the business world and also for successful performance. In the same vein, entrepreneurs who come out ahead tend to attribute the cause of their success to their actions and their management. For the most part those who fail, don't.

Viktor Frankl (1946), one of the great defenders of freedom for human beings, clearly indicated its influence in his book, *Man's Search for Meaning*. This author, who spent two years at Auschwitz and Dachau concentration camps and who lost his entire family in the Holocaust, said, "they can lock you up in a prison, but nobody can take away your freedom to choose your attitude to the things that are happening to you [...]. The prisoner who lost his faith in the future – in his future – was doomed. With his loss of faith in the future he also lost his spiritual support; he let himself go, fell apart and became the subject of physical and spiritual annihilation. As a general rule this soon gave rise to a form of crisis, the symptoms of which were familiar to anyone with experience of the camps." So these prisoners lost hope and the conviction that it was worth the trouble to keep fighting.

Special attention should be paid to the relevance of this causality relationship on people who have power. We all know the quotation, "Great power brings great responsibilty." It was the maxim in the last vignette of the first story published about Spiderman. This kind of responsibility falls on the shoulders of all those in power – be it great or small – and each in his or her own position: senior management, certainly, but also leaders of small teams. All must accept responsibility for their actions and, of course, for their failures to act. An external locus of control may be very dangerous in their hands.

Figure 9.1 Responsibility and Locus of Control

"Great power brings great responsibility."

How is this related to innovative behaviour? These thoughts emphasise the need for members of an organization to understand the value of their personal creative efforts within new idea-generating machinery. This is the only way they will consciously and unconsciously contribute all of their creativity.

1.2. Orientation to Learning Goals

According to the well-known American psychologist Edwin A. Locke (1968), goals or aims are "that which an individual strives to achieve, it is the objective or the purpose of an action". In other words, they are a movement engine and a guide for our actions given that they condition what we will and won't do, as well as the effort we will devote to a task.

Goals are the central pillar of the theory created by Dweck and Reppucci (1973). These two educational psychologists designed their first experimental work by interweaving sessions with an experimenter who provided subjects with easy problems and with those of another collaborator who provided problems that were impossible to solve. Their discovery took place after proving, in the presence of the "failure experimenter", that some students were unable to solve some very simple problems that they had previously been given by the "success experimenter" and that had already been easily solved. These students had resigned themselves to failure in his presence.

The research showed that the students were divided into two groups. The first group were students who were "execution orientated", who when faced with difficult tasks, felt anxious and lost interest and confidence in their ability to perform the tasks. This was accompanied by feelings of pessimism and sadness. These students sought to show off their skills in school, and to be rewarded for them. The second group consisted of students who were "learning orientated" – students who used school as an opportunity to learn, increase their own skills and boost their abilities. These students saw the problems as challenges, and for them, internal motivation was the main action engine.

Although this theory emerged as a result of research using schoolchildren as subjects, subsequent research showed that it can be extrapolated and applied in the framework of other disciplines such as social, clinical and health psychology, but also in sport and the work environment (Vandewalle, 2001).

In actual fact, in the business field, "learning orientated" people tend to have a more proactive attitude and better receptivity to constructive criticism from their colleagues. They are the people who generate more information and do more to spread it around (Sinkula *et al.,* 1997). However, in addition to this, "learning orientation" is also found in the field of innovation, where it is seen as an essential factor for ensuring the fluidity of the process (Kast, 1979).

Nevertheless, the benefits go much further than that. Neurons are the basic cells of the brain and they specialize in the reception and transmission of information. Until relatively recently, it was thought that once the brain had formed, its cells could no longer regenerate or reproduce. People thought they were born with a set number of neurons and that with time, little by little, they lost them. In some persons, factors such as drugs or alcohol, accidents or disease accelerates this process of brain death with devastating consequences.

In contrast to this traditional and almost unquestioned attitude, Ramón y Cajal (Nobel Prize for Medicine, 1906) mooted neuronal regeneration almost a century ago. This celebrated doctor published a number of articles supporting the theory summed up in his work, *Studies on the degeneration and regeneration of the nervous system*. Alas, the fact that he was almost a century ahead of his time meant that his revolutionary view could proceed no further.

However, recent research demonstrates this regeneration, known as neurogenesis. These discoveries have opened a door of hope in the treatment of diseases such as Parkinson's and Alzheimer's. By way of example, Magavi and his co-workers (2000) demonstrated this process in their experiments with rats. Gould and his team (1999) showed it in adult primates. These are not the only ones, and now hardly anyone dares question these promising theories.

Having come so far, the next question is inevitable: What does all this have to do with innovation? Have we lost the thread of this chapter? No, we certainly have not.

Many people come to work seeking to show that they are excellent workers and can do things well ("execution orientated"). For these people, innovation always represents the risk of failure but it also means that doing the same things as they always did and following the pathway that always worked stands in the way of their desire to shine. Innovation requires an attitude orientated towards learning, one that sees goals as challenges and a source of knowledge and skill development. This implies the need for a change of "mental software" for many, which calls for a significant effort on their part. This leads them to ask themselves, "Why do it? Why make an effort to learn? What does the company have to innovate for?"

If we take a good, hard look at the effect which this learning process will have on each one of us, we see that we are the main beneficiaries of this change of chip. According to recent research, the final stage of the learning process stimulates the process of neurogenesis, that is, neuron regeneration (Döbrössy *et al.*, 2003). Doesn't that look like a good option? You certainly couldn't find a cheaper medicine.

Let me conclude this section with a few lines about the central pillar of Socrates' words, "Know thyself," the sentence that stood at the gate of the temple of the Oracle of Delphos, sacred site to which the Greeks went to consult the gods.

It is important to learn new things every day: technical know-how, lessons from things that went wrong, how to do things better, etc. But the most effective learning takes place after your "destructure" – the breaking down of old knowledge, patterns, mechanics, etc. – and the subsequent restructure from new perspectives. What are my weaknesses? What are my strengths? Where are my limitations and my automatic mechanisms? What are my false perceptions and what responsibilities have I failed to shoulder? How do I project myself to others? We dare not forget this if we wish to lead in the new era. Innovation, change and transformation have to begin in each one of us.

2. Innova 3DX for the Psychological Profile (II)

Personality traits (optimism, self-esteem, locus of control and orientation towards learning) are very important in the world of innovation, and are alone responsible for some 15 – 20 per cent of a person's behaviour. Let's look at the effects of the locus of control and orientation towards learning.

If we don't feel in charge of our lives and are also unwilling to learn, we'll block the innovative impulses that reach us. If I believe that the strings that control my life are in the hands of others, if my desire is to remain within my comfort zone, never take a chance, never feel scared, and always do things the way they have always been done, what is going to happen if I sense an innovative impulse? I'll have to redirect it towards the usual action area, avoid making any effort, and rely on the efficiency of repetition. I may even manage to do things a shade faster, perhaps by streamlining an action, but this is not real innovation.

This means that professionals who aspire to lead in the field of innovation as entrepreneurs, or, indeed, as team leaders, must make sure that they take responsibility for all their actions, and are aware of the importance of learning (and understanding yourself) to give 100 per cent.

Figure 9.2 Locus of Control and Orientation Towards Learning Test

Instructions: score your opinion on each statement from 0 – to 10, with 0 being the lowest score and 10 the highest. You may use decimals if you wish.

Locus of control (questions designed on the basis of the Rotter scale, 1966).		
1.	In the long run, success is a question of hard work.	— —, —
2.	The future is not cast in stone.	— —, —
3.	Time is the master and puts us all in our places.	— —, —
4.	I am in control of the course my life will follow.	— —, —
5.	I feel responsible for my actions.	— —, —
Average score		— —, —

Orientation towards learning (questions designed on the basis of the VandeWalle scale, 2001)		
1.	I enjoy tasks which involve challenges.	— —, —
2.	I like it when I'm assigned duties that mean I will learn something.	— —, —
3.	I seek activities that give me a chance to learn.	— —, —
4.	In the workplace, I need activities that give me a chance to learn.	— —, —
5.	It's worth taking a risk to develop my know-how.	— —, —
Average score		— —, —

Result: from 0 – 3.5 (inclusive) very low, from 3.5 – 5 (inclusive) low, from 5 – 6.5 (inclusive) adequate, from 6.5 – 10 (inclusive) very high.

Figure 9.3 Psychological Profile Quadrant (II)

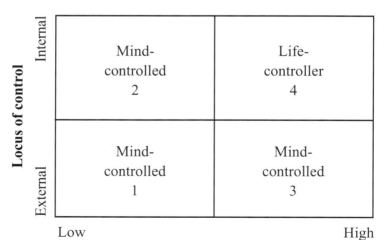

167

In quadrant no.4 we find those who feel responsible for their lives and want more; they need to learn and experience new things. They are not dominated by their minds; rather, they govern their own thoughts and actions. They are the "life-controllers".

In the other quadrants we find the "mind-controlled", those who are dominated by the thought that we are not responsible for our actions and who are therefore defined by other people. They are the ones who always want to do things the same way because it gives them a comfort zone that makes them feel calm.

3. Insight Management, Locus of Control and Orientation Towards Learning

So far we've focused on identity, self-esteem and simply being powerful, so the next step is to learn to exercise this power, which means enjoying your capacity for actions that produce and achieve dreams. So far, so good, but what follows, as many will understand, is responsibility for your actions. Taking hold of the tiller of your life will sometimes mean getting lost or making mistakes. Every sailor knows that. If you aren't prepared to grasp it, then don't travel, but you have to be aware of the fact that sparing yourself gives rise to the problem, as Benedetti brilliantly puts it, of "remaining motionless, our joy frozen, loving with distaste, our sleep dreamless" (from the poem, "Don't spare yourself").

The locus of control implies the sensation of steering your own life, pushing the tiller this way and that, depending on whatever you decide at any given moment. The first thing you have to do is decide that you are aware of the fact that you can choose, because if not, you will pass through life fulfilling other people's wishes – those of your parents, your partner, your children, your boss, etc. Your own desires may be a long way from theirs, to be a firefighter or a gardener, to dance salsa or learn to cook.

You must never let anybody drive you away from what you want to experience. If you do, you'll turn into a grey person – extinguished, irritable and misunderstood.

While you enjoy the privilege of being alive, you can ask yourself these questions. Am I in charge of my life? Who has power over me? To whom shall I yield my power? Do I live in the present? Do my past successes or my hope for the future guarantee anything?

> "If you follow your destiny, you will survive, if you live in the eternal present, you will not die."
>
> *Tao Te Ching*

I worked with a manager in Barcelona who made a particular impression on me because he was making €300,000 a year and that had left him in a state of perpetual fear that he might lose his job/salary and find himself in difficulties. There is no shortage of people who would be very pleased to make that sum in 10 years rather than in 1 and would feel no fear if they could just do it once. We observed what was happening and attempted to approach his reality without imposing any pre-judgements. We started by trying to find out if he actually *liked* his job, and came to the conclusion that it was not so much fear he felt but desire. He found it difficult to bear the situation internally because he *didn't like* the job, the environment or the prospects, but he couldn't let go of it because his fear of unemployment and being in want was so great.

We then worked on what his being let go would actually mean, since the market was actually going nowhere and there were demands on him that were all but impossible to achieve. He felt that to not achieve would mean he'd failed, which would cause a huge blow to his ego and self-image. His self-esteem was already diminishing because he felt worthless, and thought nobody would take him on afterwards. Little by little, we unpicked the

Gordian knots that he thought impossible to undo. In the end, he changed jobs because he wanted to; he wasn't let go. That made him quite happy. He earned less but it didn't affect his self-esteem. Granting himself permission to be outside of what everyone expected provided him with a vital opportunity that he would have wasted otherwise – while earning a fortune and constantly being in the grip of fear.

Are you afraid of making mistakes? It's actually inevitable, and it might be interesting to explore it, since there's no reason to become blocked because of it. A lot is said about how in a crisis you have to embrace change, change management, etc., but when it's your turn, the initial response is almost always "no", and the second might be, "well, if I can't avoid it, let's analyse how, when and in what direction". Too often "analysis + analysis = paralysis".

Not long ago my mother telephoned to say that there was a film on television based on my great-grandmother. Interested, I turned on the television and saw a woman, who, having failed to find her right place in life, decided to take the veil and become a nun. In the process, she discovered her vocation to help others, worked with a doctor, and inspired everybody with her wit and passion. However, her confessor, suspecting something unusual was happening, tried to get her removed from the hospital and away from the doctor before she took her perpetual vows. The effect was instant: doctor and nun were now totally changed. The separation made him very nervous and her very depressed. Thanks to her confessor's nudging, she decided to give up being a nun. The result was that the doctor lost a collaborating nun and gained a wife and a son – my grandfather.

I'm impressed by the strength and drive of people like her, who don't have the advantage of 15 years in analysis and don't need the spur of being let go in order to move, yet they succeed in making the changes their lives require in order to find themselves.

"Invest in losses" is the old Taoist saying, which means selling even when you're sure to lose in order to carry on with life and the new things it brings.

If someone says, "Hey, here I am! I'm not scared, but I don't know which way to go!". Don't worry, it doesn't matter, first just get moving and then you can see if you want to change direction. Movement first, awareness second.

Another factor operating here is that when someone does try to act outside of their programming to do something else, they tend to copy others, and that doesn't do them any good. Where others have triumphed by means of certain manoeuvres, others will experience glorious collapse. Nadal possesses some strokes which, with his makeup, stature, character and determination make him a master, but others should not follow him down this road. Only the movements that emerge from the true inner master are successful. Lessons from other people are useful for learning something about a medium, getting to know the enemy, etc., but can't guarantee future upcoming battles.

As Claudio Naranjo explains so eruditely and wisely, self-knowledge helps to "remove the veil" as the mystics put it, and leads to a clearer perception of your reality and that of others. This makes the way of relating to it so much more efficient. All learning, particularly self-learning, must be focused not so much on a goal as on a path where experience and knowledge constantly follow each other. If you focus on knowledge as the goal you'll never achieve it. I have friends who are eternally hooked on a range of unsatisfactory therapies because they set it as a goal and not a journey. This journey is the length of a life. Those who believe that they have reached the end of the road have merely spared themselves and gone to sleep; are no longer looking, no longer learning, no longer living and no longer steering.

Solid self-knowledge gives you the opportunity to choose your own path, the one that keeps you alive and feeling passionate and in control. Don't be a victim, decide about your own life. Now more than ever there are well-trained and supervised therapists within reach who will help you understand the feelings that Viktor Frankl talked about: being in control, feeling powerful, full and optimistic.

One last question: should you approach life in a spirit of confidence and devotion, or in a spirit that's distrustful and suspicious? When I was a teenager I came home from school one day, my mother opened the door looking like the perfect loving and nourishing mum, gave me a big smile, and just as I was about to kiss her on the cheek she whipped out a saucepan from behind her back and hit me over the head with it, saying something that I'll never forget, "Never trust anyone, not even your mother!" and then she burst out laughing, as if she were some illuminated Zen teacher.

This is a "Zen stick" that at the time I didn't understand. Allow me to explain: however much I try to develop trust in life, I still believe you have to keep your eyes open. In these uncaring times it is particularly important.

A few recent examples of micro to macro will serve: I go to the butcher and ask for four steaks and when I get home I find two are good and two have gone off. My restaurant bill charges for two extra dishes. The shoe-shop owner is selling up to retire and sells me a pair of €6 baby shoes at a sale price of nearly €8! The telephone company and the bank both charge me for services I don't use and getting the money back costs so much in money and trouble it would just be easier to pay up. I used to have a very high level job at a very well-known company that gave me a huge office but no contract because they didn't want to pay Social Security. I bought a house with a garage, but when I'd paid they told me I had no access to bring the car in or out over the pavement.

I realise that this is news to no-one and that everybody could add a good few more anecdotes to the list, and indeed, it might do them good. So perhaps we should burn the lengthy list and dance around the flames, in an effort to exorcise the feelings of aggression, deception, anger, disenchantment, sadness, impotence, etc., which is constantly generated in our faces and indeed on all sides. It might be more therapeutic than a game of football, a Champions final, for example, and we could to it much more often.

Why do all these businessmen and businesses take such risks? Is it worth the trouble? What has happened to best practices? Where did ethics and conscience go? What is social responsibility and corporate social responsibility? I've stopped wondering what will become of our children – I'm wondering what will become of us.

Krishnamurti said that being well adapted to a sick society meant that you had to be sick, too. Winning like this is like succeeding at being a lunatic among lunatics. Brilliant foolishness. The system that governs today leads you to think that being mad and winning, as I've described above, or sucking people and resources dry is the good life, but don't be deceived. This is bread for today and hunger for tomorrow, leaving great damage along the way. I'm saying this for those who believe in the existence of sin or karma.

Focus on responsibility as your demonstration of control. If you break china, pay for it and carry on in control with a lesson well learnt. The individual is bound to feel indignant, like the Spanish *indignados* protesting against unemployment, but don't confuse the two; being indignant has no connection with any particular political party even though many try to profit from this point of view. Being indignant means having had enough, being fed up and loaded with frustration, anger and a pressing need for change. If you're tired of feeling passively furious, then get up and act indignant.

My recommendation is that as people, businesses and institutions, you invest in quality, honesty and trust – to ensure that people are happy, not stressed out and not always on the run from aggression. If you do this, your customers will stay with you even if you charge them a little more, because they will be calm, certain that they are never going to be clouted on the head with a saucepan. The same goes for your staff: organize things so that they can develop their talent and career with you, because they will then feel at ease in the company being supported by you; they will not look at other companies, nor will they steal your human capital. Try to invest in your customers, too, not just in your marketing; indeed, you should internalise your own image campaigns and turn them into reality. Comply. Generate trust.

10
Passion for Innovation. First Factor: Motivation

1. Motivation and its Movement Mechanism

1.1. Motivational Impulses

The word motivation derives from the Latin *motivus,* meaning the cause of movement. Former athlete and American politician Jim Ryun is the creator of a statement that accurately explains why it is essential to the innovative process, "Motivation is what gets you started. Habit is what keeps you going."

A number of explanations have been offered on the motivation-action sequence. They seek to answer such questions such as: Why is it that something motivates us, or indeed, what is it that demotivates us? What are the keys needed to turn motivation into passion? All the explanations have made interesting contributions but none have succeeded in assuming a universal application, as it would probably seem too simplistic. Nevertheless, it is important to be familiar with them, since they help to explain our behaviour.

Edward Lee Thorndike (1911) is one of the pioneers in the study of motivation. His research using maze boxes are very well-known. These studies allowed Thorndike to observe that behaviour which is rewarded tends to become imprinted as learnt behaviour, while that which produces an unrewarding or irritating situation tends to become eliminated. This led him to frame his Law of Effect which states that we all tend to repeat actions for which we have received a reward, and to avoid those for which we have received punishment.

The years between 1940 and 1960 were a very fruitful period in this field. During this period theories were advanced that came under serious attack, yet are still the best known theories about why we perform an action. Some of the best known ones are Abraham Maslow's Hierarchy of Needs and the X and Y theories of Douglas McGregor.

Maslow (1943) saw man as a "perpetually wanting animal" moved by a pyramid of needs: physiological (food, shelter) safety (protection from physical and emotion harm), social (affection, friendship), self-esteem (status, recognition) and fulfilment (growth, achievement of potential). He sought to satisfy them in ascending order, and then ceased to be motivated once they are satisfied. He thus provided us with an interesting foundation for understanding behaviour, but he committed a serious error in his interpretation of nature, given that human beings almost always want more.

Figure 10.1 Maslow's Pyramid

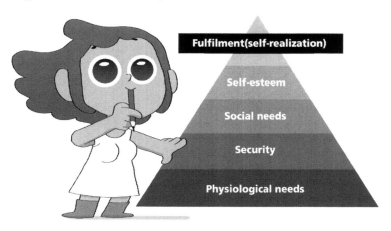

McGregor (1960) studied the implications of Maslow's theory in organizations and expressed his conclusions on the X & Y theories. His X theory assumed that people avoid work, which means that they have to be controlled, directed and even threatened. Under this management style, motivation arises from fear and threats. Alternatively we have the Y theory which assumes that people like to work, that they are capable of directing themselves and that they want (and need) to assume responsibilities. This focus also stated that people are creative and that their intellectual capacities can be very valuable. The work showed that traditional management theories are all too often based on supposition X. This led McGregor to become a firm defender of the second perception, and he made a very significant effort to demonstrate that human capital can help companies achieve their goals.

Both theories are very well known nowadays, but they have suffered the effects of in-depth examination aimed at testing their validity in the field of work. This has led to the development of new explanations that provide more modern reasoning, although some of them are already several decades old. Worthy of note among them are: David McClelland's theory of the Three Needs, B. F. Skinner's theory of Positive Reinforcement, Edwin Locke's theory of Goal Setting and Victor Vroom's theory of Expectancy.

McClelland (1961) demonstrates that three acquired (not innate) needs exist: needs for achievement, power and affiliation. We all share these needs; what differentiates us is how they affect us; in other words, their motivational impulses. If we take this theory a little further, we see that high productivity appears as a result of a match between work and the way these three needs manifest in each individual. McClelland paid special attention to the need for success, understood as striving and the desire to do things better and indeed to achieve excellence. He saw this need as a potent driver or biological engine that selects, activates and directs behaviour. According to his research, people with a strong need for success prefer activities that provide challenge – moderately difficult tasks (as opposed to very easy or very difficult tasks), for which they are responsible for the outcome.

Skinner's theory of Positive Reinforcement (1974) was formulated on the basis of Edward Lee Thorndike's work. Skinner's Law of Reinforcement states that our behaviour can become strengthened or weakened as a function of what follows. Positive reinforcement strengthens it, while the elimination of positive reinforcement weakens it. This theory also postulates that punishment helps to reduce a given behaviour, but it does not teach new ones. The main limitation of this theory is that it takes no account of a person's internal state. This leads to one of the most questioned aspects of his thesis – being the transfer that produces the process of animal learning within the human.

Edwin Locke's theory of Goal Setting (1968) explains cognitive motivation, understood as behaviour that is guided or directed by a mental representation (cognition) of the future. It suggests that people actively seek to achieve goals and objectives, since this gives meaning to their existence and orientates their behaviour. According to this theory, goals are an important motivational tool. Its impact has been so powerful in the field of work that it has generated a new and extensively used management model, known as management by objectives.

And lastly we come to Victor Vroom's Expectancy Theory (1964) which is based on the assumption that we act seeking to maximise expected rewards. This turns our expectations of output and reward into the determining elements of motivation. In other words, the degree of motivation to perform an action is a function of the certainty that this action will allow us to achieve the desired outcome and of the value that is attributed to the result of this effort. Consequently, the greater the expectancy of probability and value of result, the greater the effort made.

Hence an historical survey of motivational impulses will reveal, among other things, reinforcement and rewards, needs, goals and expectations. This will inevitably lead to the following question: what are the drivers that really determine our motivation for innovation? What are the factors that turn motivation into passion? In this area, we must concentrate on expectations, in particular.

1.2. Motivational Expectations

The origin of Victor Vroom's Expectancy Theory (1964) is the work of Edward Lee Thorndike (1874-1949), beyond a doubt one of the main researchers the US has produced in the study of behaviour. This being the case, we shall dedicate a few lines in this section to one of his major sources of inspiration.

Thorndike is particularly well-known for the experiments he performed using reward chambers (maze boxes, later Skinner boxes) where he analysed the strategies adopted by various species to solve problems. He observed that when an animal performed an action by chance, such as pressing a lever, and it was accompanied by a pleasant reward for the creature, such as getting out of the cage and a treat, the behaviour was repeated.

Thanks to this observation, in 1911 he was able to frame his famous Law of Effect, "Of the various responses which are available in the same situation and under the same conditions, those responses which are accompanied or immediately followed by the animal's satisfaction will remain more firmly connected with the situation, such that when this takes place again, the said responses will have a greater likelihood of occurring; those responses which are accompanied or immediately followed by an unpleasant feeling for the animal, all other conditions remaining constant, will have weakened its connections with the said situation, such that when this situation is repeated, the said responses will have a lower likelihood of occurring. The greater the satisfaction or the discomfort, the greater will be the reinforcement of the union." In short, he had scientifically demonstrated the power of reward.

This theory has been extensively and thoroughly applied in a number of fields, including business, where researchers following Victor Vroom have developed their own theories, seeking a universal formula for motivation. This has not yet been found, but thanks to these researchers' efforts, we come a little closer every day to understanding its operating mechanisms.

Vroom's Expectancy Theory postulates that the degree of motivation to perform a given action is the result of the interaction of two elements: expectancy that if it's performed it will be rewarded, and the value attributed to the desired reward. Extrapolating this to Thorndike's theory, it would represent the relationship between the lever and the door opening.

In more concrete terms, motivation depends initially on the causal relationship between the effort that must be made and the result that we hope to achieve. This element is of a cognitive nature, reflecting the subjective perception (or conviction) that a real link exists between them. These expectancies are formed for the most part as a result of our own previous experience and those of others.

As an example, what would your reaction be if the company "asks" you to make an extraordinary effort because without that effort they won't achieve the commercial results they set as their quarterly goal?

Suppose this quarter that extraordinary effort has been made to sell projects, but the market was not receptive. The commercial proposal didn't seem to "take" – the product wasn't well received. You would think you couldn't do anything about it. In other words, your result expectancy would be close to zero.

Are you going to make that extraordinary effort? Perhaps you'd make one last try (everything for the cause), but with little hope. In fact, even if you did it, you'd certainly not place much expectancy on your effort, and this would not go unnoticed by the customer, dooming the outcome.

The second element, the value of the result (also known as valence), refers to the valuation each one makes about what is hoped to be achieved. It covers the intensity of individual attraction felt regarding a given result. This is a subjective force that is conditioned by the degree to which it satisfies desires or needs. Kurt Zadek Lewin (1890-1947), by whom Vroom was inspired while developing his concept, explained it in his theory of human personality. He proposed a new reading and explanation for behaviour by applying the laws of contemporary physics, more specifically in the field of force. As a result, for Lewin (1935), "the valence of an object usually derives from the fact that the goal is a means to the satisfaction of a need, or has indirectly something to do with the satisfaction of a need".

Now imagine that you are being offered an exotic holiday (you can choose the destination) with your partner. Will you make the same effort? Will you be equally motivated? The likelihood is that you'd find a last bit of strength where you thought none was left, and put your shoulder to the wheel. You will surely come up with something.

Let's give our imagination free rein. What would happen if they told you that if you succeeded they would give you the promotion you'd wanted for so long? Suppose that this promotion does not just mean recognition and greater power (for those who want it), but comes with a delicious rise in salary What would your reaction be? Would you sweat blood? I bet you would, but the effort wouldn't end there. You'd give it absolutely everything you had.

In brief, motivation for a given action is determined by the expectancy that the effort will be of use, and that there is a value for each of us in the result.

Why does it happen? The answer is endorphins.

These hormones have a crucial part to play in how we feel every moment of every day. Once secreted, they act as natural analgesics and intoxicants, making a profound effect on happiness. The effect is similar to that of morphine, but much more powerful. Nor do they cause the damage that narcotics do, since they are a substance generated by your own body. Coming back to Victor Vroom's theory, expectancies generate endorphins and they motivate us.

Having come thus far, it is important to add a critical hint . What motivates us is not directly expectancy but rather the emotions they generate. In other words, for the same expectancy, if the emotional effect is different, the motivation will also change.

Suppose the company announces a promotion *plus* a 50 per cent salary rise to the person who wins the "Idea of the Year" competition. Will you be motivated? If you wish to remain in your comfort zone, will you be attracted by the idea of winning? It could be that even thinking about the possibility makes you anxious; even so, the more ambitious spirits will feel very happy at the idea of possible victory. So the same reward motivates and demotivates, depending on the individual's internal state and as a function of the emotions he or she is capable of feeling. This means that managing expectancies cannot remain at a superficial level, with probability or value; the emotional effect must be factored in (and managed).

Proving the Expectancy Theory has run into a number of methodological difficulties which have shown that it must be handled with care. Because it was successfully applied in a number of research programmes, there have been no shortage of critics questioning its messages. Nevertheless, rather than totally invalidating the theory, what's been achieved is a validation for those situations where we can clearly perceive the connection between effort and outcome. This means that the theory appears rather idealistic in some situations, throwing light on how to motivate staff which then leads to deliberate efforts to buttress the link between effort and reward.

Figure 10.2 Motivational Expectancies

How does this affect the field of innovation? Our level of motivation is the result of emotions generated by hopes that we will be successful if we make the effort, and, of course, our assessment that this will be of value.

Before concluding this section I want to comment about the initiatives found in Germany and China in this area. In Germany, the Law on Employee Inventions recognizes the right to receive compensation for workplace innovations. But it is China that has led in the paradigm change field, with patent legislation which gives employees a (reasonable) reward of two per cent of the profit generated by the application of the patent and 10 per cent of the licences. Would we be equally motivated to innovate if such a law applied in our country? Whatever the situation, be it growth or crisis, the answer is obvious – the application of the law would establish a "before and after" situation.

2. Innova 3DX for Motivation

Motivational expectancies normally generate around 20 per cent of innovative behaviour in both genders, which means they play a crucial role in management. I want to draw attention to the rather low score it receives in surveys: low expectancies on results and low valuation as regards reward. I've observed this in large corporation and in SMEs, in public and private sectors.

Bad news? On the contrary, these results turn the two ingredients of this theory into an effective lever for stimulating innovative behaviour.

What can you do if your teams feel incapable of innovation? What can you do if, to the contrary, the problem is that people already see that it may be a waste of time? Worse still, what can be done if past experiences lead people to think that the only person to profit by innovation is the boss? Or some much "smarter" work colleague?

A satisfactory communication policy and some clear recognition and reward mechanisms could lead to a 180 degree turnaround in a very short time, but it could also help consolidate a change that could persist as part of the strategy. Every business has to fine-tune its levers and define its own operational pathways, but after many years of research, I find myself in no doubt that for a great many people this will be their most reliable and profitable action.

Figure 10.3 Motivational Expectancies Test

To measure expectancies we have taken ten items worked out on the basis of the contributions of Smith, *et al.* (2008):

Instructions: score your opinion on each statement from 0 – 10, with 0 the lowest score and 10 the highest. You may use decimals if you wish.

Expectancies of probability		
1.	I am capable of innovation.	— —, —
2.	Everybody is capable of innovation.	— —, —
3.	I find it easy to innovate.	— —, —
4.	It is possible to innovate in my company.	— —, —
5.	It's easy to innovate in my company.	— —, —
Average score		— —, —
Expectations of value		
1.	Innovative effort is quickly rewarded.	— —, —
2.	It's worth the trouble to innovate.	— —, —
3.	Innovation can help me advance on a personal level.	— —, —
4.	Innovation can help me advance on a professional level.	— —, —
5.	Innovation is profitable for the innovator.	— —, —
Average score		— —, —

Result: from 0 – 3.5 (inclusive) very low, from 3.5 – 5 (inclusive) low, from 5 – 6.5 (inclusive) adequate, from 6.5 – 10 (inclusive) very high.

Figure 10.4 Motivational Expectancies Quadrant

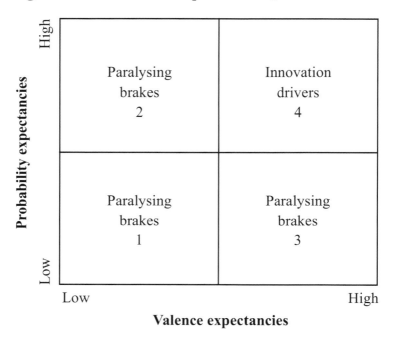

In the fourth quadrant both expectations act as engines driving subjects towards innovation, so they behave as innovation drivers.

In the other quadrants, however, expectancies act as "paralysing brakes". In these cases the creative impulse is in danger of being extinguished or of simply never appearing again. If this is your case or that of your team or business ... don't waste a second. This is the place to start effecting change.

3. Insight Management and Motivation

Motivation is something that arises from inside or outside. If it's your job to motivate others, then you should take these lines to heart, because the fate of your team is in your hands.

If, however, other people take it upon themselves to motivate you, then don't just relax, check on how to maintain your own intrinsic motivation so as not to run out of steam halfway up the mountain.

When you climb that mountain, you want to give the ground a good thump while you advance – go on, make it and your own body shake. This is not a metaphor – stamp on the ground, the piano, the ball, move your hips, dance, vibrate, resound, stay alive with intensity and passion, with rhythm, with love and hate if you have to, as long as it's vibrant and motivated. My initial approach to the subject is therefore bioenergetic. If your body doesn't produce adrenalin and endorphins – if you're not creating your own drugs, you'll become disheartened and unable to face the big challenges because your body will simply not respond.

Then be very careful about where you place your energy, because it's limited. If you commit yourself to a project, don't bother planning escape routes because you'll lose the strength you need to tackle what you're actually doing. Carefully take aim and fire at the desired bull's-eye. If you're unable to commit yourself, you'll miss. If you need the job although you don't believe in it, work out the motivations that you need: money, social recognition, your partner's or your parents' or children's respect. Whatever you do, don't stay at home getting depressed, etc. Do whatever it takes – but do it in stages. There's nothing worse than swimming in the ocean without knowing if you'll ever make it to a beach where you can rest. You could drown.

A businessman consulted me on a matter that had to do with his wife. He believed their relationship was in crisis, while what was really happening was that he was competing for a promotion and had lost his motivation. He was so exhausted by the tremendous and prolonged effort that he had become careless about himself and had been neglecting his wife. He was in urgent need of a dream, a way out of his boring life – some kind of adventure, something illicit and pleasurable. In his case there was no need to plunge into a long course of therapy; a simple sheet of paper with concrete daily and weekly study goals, and times for review and rest resulted in this man not only getting his breath back, and his energy, but he passed the test, re-established his relationship with his wife and there was no need for him to go seeking a lover.

If you need to trick yourself to motivate yourself and your people, do it. There's a well-known folktale about a trickster shaman. The man arrives in a village in serious need of food, and having no money, calls on the children of the village to help him make a stew out of stones. The children, fascinated by the trickster's magic, hurry to do what he wants them to, to see this magic, and he in turn lights a fire and places a pot full of water on it to boil. He then takes out some "magic" stones he has in his bag and puts them into the water. The children watch in amazement as it boils, and the man remarks that the stew would be much richer if they put something in it to give it a little flavour. The children run to their homes and each one brings something back: potatoes, sausage, ham, turnip greens, etc. They're all fascinated by the magic that they're all helping to create. Very soon the stew's ready and they all share it, laughing, feeling like fellow conspirators, united, happy, and with full bellies. The shaman, who then saves the stones for the next occasion, had played a trick on them – and succeeded not only in getting a free meal, but also in imparting a magical experience to the children that was redolent of wit and passion.

There are many theories about motivation, there are numerous pathways and no particular model will guarantee success. This means that you have to advance in your own way. What motivated you once may no longer work and what is good for one person might be no good for somebody else. Finding out how other people motivate themselves may provide a hint, but each individual has to find their own way, and this will often include a mixture of success, expectations, emotions, supports and possibly other factors.

The theory of expectations is of special importance for one reason: awareness. An expectation improvement system is of no use if the person seeking motivation is not aware of what it implies for them, or what they might win or lose. It's one thing to place a prize on the table, quite another to put a value on that prize. If you really don't understand the repercussions your action will have, you aren't really taking part. Look at it from the opposite angle: if we all understood the repercussions of emitting pollution all over the planet and perpetuating poverty in the world, the motivation for our actions to change that would be of the highest order. But if we aren't aware, our motivation is abstract and fades like smoke from the burning Amazon forest.

In the business world the most powerful motivation can very often be a mental image, an expectation that helps, and then generates the desire to achieve it: a bonus, a prize holiday which you've set your heart on, some evidence of recognition, etc. In all these cases, dangling the carrot in front of the hungry donkey works, but if the donkey isn't hungry, it doesn't.

Coming back to a holistic viewpoint, although the mental and the emotional go hand-in-hand, I like to feel that vibration rise from below and spread throughout the entire body. I see it as much more powerful and lasting. The mental image is also stimulating, but I forget, I can easily be distracted by something else, taking it as normal, ceasing to assign value to it. I can even become demotivated if the extraordinary prize vanishes. That's why I prefer to reassess emotion as energy, movement and direction, so that I can take advantage of it as a leader or as an individual.

Passion is the pulse that not only allows you to be alive, but gives you the desire to keep on battling, developing and creating. Without it, there is nothing, since you cease to live in the present then, and your gaze towards the future is lost. Having hope and heightened emotion for a project generates energy that feeds back into work, nourishing and teaching you. Passion is contagious, as is lethargy.

Unfortunately, lethargy and envy are powerful allies against passion and innovation. If you have to put up with a reasonable period of time stuck in the desert, where you feel alone, not just because nobody is backing you, but because they're sapping your strength and motivation, cling to impeccability, a profound and powerful concept much appreciated by the shamans and reflected in the works of Carlos Castaneda, the well-known Mexican healer Pachita and others. To boost and maintain motivation it's important to be impeccable in important areas such as your love of work or of a job well done, and to work without needing to be appreciated by others. This attitude is most obvious because of its absence in the modern world, where customers and employees are burnt like forests are burnt, having childishly believed that all those resources were infinite.

When I was a child, I got a great lesson from reading Michael Ende's novel *Momo*. One of the characters was a sweeper, who explained to the girl, Momo, that he would carefully sweep the great square of the city every day from early morning, even though it was huge and the result wouldn't last, and even though there would be no round of applause for him at the end. He did his job by ensuring that each flagstone, one by one, was immaculate, never looking to see how many he had left to do, and so he went home happy when he had finished. I still feel that it's an admirable attitude and the best way for each of us to do our own particular job.

Let's go back to emotion-movement (they come from the same root): emotion provides or deploys a quantity of energy that is directed at an objective, which may or may not be in line with a mental goal, so aligning ourselves is very important. The relationship between emotion and motivation is two-directional, carrying one and the other and vice versa.

In terms of motivation, rivers of ink have been wasted on the theme of passion and it's obvious why. If I feel passion for something, I will vibrate, I will want it to express itself and I will be occupied and involved with it from head to toe, head over heels in fact, as those in love put it.

If you go for crazy love, then go for it in your own way, vibrating, hoping, expecting and even suffering as part of the journey. If you do things the way others want you to, you're wasting your life. No passion will come from that. Forget your parents, boss, grandfather, teacher, therapist and spiritual confessor.

Now, let's take one more step forward and then we'll undertake a brief review of the other emotions that also inject weight and motion, causing *com*motion. The first thing we have to take into account is which emotions, and in which direction their energy and intensity are moving:

In the case of fear, you have to escape what causes it. Fear that is sustained over time saps vital energy, happiness and mental clarity. People who are burdened by fear are blocked and become paranoid and can behave very aggressively. Do you work harder when you're afraid you might be sacked? It depends – you don't produce more, since part of your productive energy is needed to assess the threat and work out what to do if they *do* fire you. A person who is not afraid can focus their energy on the job.

Of course, there is another extreme: the person who is completely fearless and knows that whatever they do won't lead to repercussions can also lack motivation. I'm not suggesting a whip, but I do recommend a system of reasonable rewards and punishments. Activation in the creative process is fundamental, but if it turns into paralysing fear, then that's not good. If the threat moves you towards generating ideas then that is good.

Rage can help destroy in order to then create, although suppressing anger can lead to serious depression. However it can also help, if well focused, to produce a greater yield, like winning a tennis final in the fifth hour of the game. As far as creativity is concerned, rage is usually too powerful, like a runaway horse, breaking and knocking down things that aren't any use in order to create space. Kind of like a sledgehammer to crack a nut.

Sadness leaches away the energy of movement, but like autumn it can be an invitation to plunge deep into oneself, meditate and have some insights. Don't underestimate it, it is a hugely productive emotion if you take advantage of this emotional "water" to go with the flow, and develop fresh ideas with a cooler head. It can be essential for working at a delicate level, having less fire.

Happiness is vital not only at the social level, since it is contagious, but also for you to maintain a sustainable career. It helps you ride a wave and keep on enjoying it. Disinterested happiness, Buddhist happiness, would have more to do with serene spiritual fulfilment, which is absolutely essential for certain kinds of delicate and refined jobs. Along with this comes confidence, which is also important, because a suspicious person is reticent, reserved, distant and unable to become deeply involved in either a project or relationships. If I suspect my boss is going to steal my idea, I don't even bother to work it out.

Let's include some other phenomena that are interesting from the movement and motivation angle:

Curiosity is valuable as an aspect of proactive, forward, exploratory movement, when you search with your eyes wide open. There is no doubt that most inventions have been the result of adventurous curiosity.

Disgust is visceral, spontaneous and obviously generates repulsion, rejection and withdrawal from contact. It is essential to recognize it in order not to waste time with something that won't work. I saw this very clearly with a vegan client, a chef who had begun to work in a non-vegan restaurant. Although she tried very hard to cook meat, the result was a disaster. She was sacked, to her full agreement because she, too, had realized the mission was impossible.

Surprise implies that you should check on a movement that may have been going in the right direction and has now been aborted. It may even be an opportunity to see reality as it really is. If you can't see any difference between yesterday and today, it's because you don't see at all.

To summarise, no emotion is bad, because motion is always energy in motion, and if channelled effectively is very useful. It is important to be aware of emotion, because if it is badly channelled or denied it will not only lead to creative blocks in you and your team, but will match what traditional Chinese medicine and even our own folk wisdom says: anger affects the liver, unhappiness affects the pancreas, sadness the lungs, obsession the head, etc.

NB: I am aware of the fact that this latter part of the chapter is not for everybody, and not everyone will understand its importance. You still need a great deal of emotional intelligence to know what is happening to you, and to manage it well, but it is vital that everyone work on it, particularly those who aim to take the lead in innovative/creative processes. A couple of simple examples: if you don't manage your anger well, you will literally burn your creative teams with your verbal and even physical outrages.

And finally, to motivate yourself it is crucial to vibrate, and to achieve this I once again invoke the principles of non-intervention and non-judgement: let each individual give free rein to their passion where it is creative and where they prefer. Neither judge nor intervene when it comes to your own movement or that of others. Remember the film, *Billy Elliot*, about the boy who wanted to dance classical ballet in a depressed industrial city, this is a true example of passion shining through.

11
Passion for Innovation.
Second Factor: Fear of Failure

1. Fear, the Paralysing Agent

1.1. Fear and its Presence

Fear may be more or less visible, but it has always been and always will be present. The ancients saw fear as a punishment from the gods. In Greek mythology, Phobos and Deimos, the sons of Ares (the god of war), were the personifications of fear and terror. The Romans named them Pallor and Pavor [Terror]. Different names for versions of the same emotion. The existentialist philosopher Jean-Paul Sartre wisely said, "All humans experience fear. All. He who does not experience fear is not normal, and this has nothing to do with courage." (Delemeau, 1989) Its presence and power are such that even Franklin Roosevelt included it as one of the main pillars of his first speech (1933) after assuming the presidency, "The only thing we have to fear is fear itself."

The Latin word was *metus,* a term that reflected the circumstances which provoke terror. Its definition is: (a) an anxious perturbation of the mind because of a real or imaginary risk or harm; and (b) a feeling of suspicion or apprehension that something undesired may happen. Its synonyms are: fright, scare, panic, terror, horror, etc.

It is important to differentiate fear from anxiety. Fear develops in the presence of actual danger and is associated with the damage, or supposed damage, this threat may cause. Anxiety, on the other hand, does not arise as the result of danger or a concrete motive. It does not develop as a result of an external stressor. It comes from within.

Fear is one of the primary or basic human emotions, together with happiness, sadness and anger. These are present at birth and are always with us. Fear is an intense and unpleasant emotion that causes us to experience a change in our mental state when faced with possible danger and/or a possible negative event. Implicit in it is the feeling of uncertainty regarding our ability to deal with this danger, and this generates nervous tension and a desire to avoid it. So it is a primary, negative emotion, since it causes negative feelings and paralysis.

When fear is described in this way it may appear to be something bad. However, this is not necessarily the case. Fear has a positive side. It is an indicator that not all is well and an emotional warning sign that physical or psychological danger is near. It is an emotion that can protect us and prevent us from coming to harm. Indeed, Charles Darwin (1872) said that emotions developed because of their importance for adaptation. For him, fear was a clear survival mechanism.

In contrast to healthy fear there is pathological fear. This takes the form of unjustified alarm in regulation and/or activation. In the first case, it occurs in an excessively intense form. In the second its activation is in too low a threshold, which means that it's been triggered far too often. Naturally, it can also appear as the outcome of a distortion of reality, the product of projections or the subject's own imagination. This is the dangerous terrain of phobias.

1.2. The Fear of Failure

The fear of failure is a very present emotion in the world of business and undoubtedly one of the greatest enemies of innovation. What is it? How does it appear? How does it affect us? What is its operating mechanism?

Fear of failure can be defined as a paralysing thought that something is not going to turn out well and that will lead to negative consequences. A high level of fear of failure leads to deep thoughts of not coming up to standard. People who suffer from this are most concerned about what others say about them, so they restrict themselves and devote valuable energy to seeking excuses and justifications for their actions. Naturally, this includes their failure to act. It's an emotion that is associated with inaction, as it seeks to avoid pain derived from making a mistake.

The concept is very close to risk aversion, indeed, the dividing line between the two is often very blurred. Risk aversion reflects the attitude of all those people who prefer to undertake sure investments or business activities even though the earnings are low, rather than take a chance and make a bigger profit. In other words, for people who suffer from risk aversion, negative emotions associated with loss are much greater than what is achieved with success.

C.P. Smith's research (1969) showed that children with higher fear of failure levels are the children of mothers who have great achievement goals and the lowest assessment of their own children's capabilities. In the same vein, a great deal of research, such as that of Hassan, Inayatullah and Khalique (1977), has shown that stern, authoritarian and punitive parents bring up their children with a greater fear of failure than others. They are not the only ones, and in fact this is a subject about which a great deal could be said. What is important to realize is that our childhoods exert a very serious effect on our fear of failure, something that parents should always bear in mind if they do not want to consolidate it in their children's personality.

The technical term for a pathological fear of failure is atychiphobia, and when experienced in this form it is seen as an illness. It is defined as an abnormal, persistent and groundless fear of failure. It is obsessive, extreme and irrational when placed against the possibility that the subject could be mistaken. This is a particularly paralysing phobia. Curiously, its polar opposite also exists – the fear of success syndrome.

The level of fear of failure experienced by a management team of a company is a factor that can significantly affect its strategic goals, and hence the path chosen to achieve them. When a management committee member suffers from such a strong fear that something bad may come of attempting to innovate, clearly any attempt at innovation is doomed. Managers in these demanding times must be emotionally prepared to assess risks intelligently, and when necessary, to run them.

In other words, if a manager wishes to deploy all of the creative potential of the team, they must run the risk of failing as well, and learn to pick up the pieces after each time it happens, having learnt a fresh lesson. If that manager spends their life besieged by fear, there's no hope that the team will be otherwise.

2. Innova 3DX for the Fear of Failure

«Fear doesn't exist anywhere
except in the mind.»

Dale Carnegie

The second step is to find an explanation. If you can find out why it arises, why it invades you and paralyses you, you can reduce its intensity. Marie Curie, the only woman to have ever received two Nobel prizes actually said, "We cease to fear something which we have learnt to understand."

In this process, your breathing plays an essential part. If you can manage to control it and get it back to normal you'll have reduced the level of fear and possibly even overcome it. If you complement this with a physical activity that generates endorphins (walking or running), you can liberate the hormones that cause you to be tense.

You must do the same on the fear of failure front. The steps are to recognize it, understand it, attempt to move beyond it and then overcome it. If it forms part of your life or that of your team's, you now know how to begin: breathe.

Figure 11.1 Fear Test

To manage and monitor fear you must make use of a double measurement. First, you measure fear in general terms: Are you living with fear? Does it affect your behaviour? To what extent? Is the fear rational or out or proportion? Let's measure your orientation towards a healthy form of fear.

And second, focus your attention on fear of failure, to see if you're dealing with a form of fear that is more or less acceptable or if it occupies a central position in your life. You can work on your tolerance for failure.

Instructions: score your opinion on each statement from 0 – 10, with 0 being the lowest score and 10 the highest. You may use decimals if you wish.

Orientation towards healthy fear		
1.	I am aware of my fears.	__ __ , __
2.	I can recognize my fears.	__ __ , __

3.	I do not allow myself to be carried away by my fears.	— — , —
4.	I do not live with fear.	— — , —
5.	I learn a great deal from my fears.	— — , —
Average score		— — , —
Tolerance for failure		
1.	Failure is part of the road to success.	— — , —
2.	After failure come successes.	— — , —
3.	Failure is a risk that has to be taken.	— — , —
4.	I have learnt a great deal from my failures.	— — , —
5.	I feel no fear of the possibility of making a mistake.	— — , —
Average score		— — , —

Result: from 0 – 3.5 (inclusive) very low, from 3.5 – 5 (inclusive) low, from 5 – 6.5 (inclusive) adequate, from 6.5 – 10 (inclusive) very high.

Figure 11.2 The Fear of Failure Quadrant

Figure 11.2 The Fear of Failure Quadrant

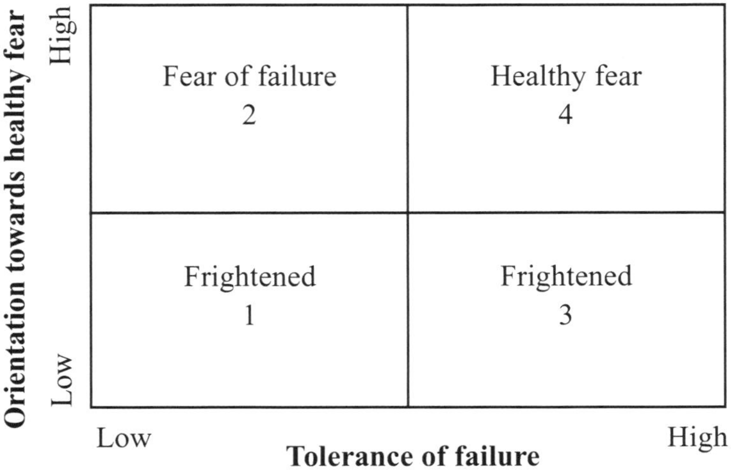

In the first and third quadrants you'll find "frightened" people, people who experience a great deal of fear that holds them back and drains their alertness and energy. Next to them, in the second quadrant, you'll find people who are blocked by their "fear of failure". If you form a part of these groups, then you know where to start.

Fear is human, but allowing yourself to be devastated by it is not. Don't waste your adrenalin, it has a much more valuable function. It develops into "healthy fear" (quadrant four). You will find that much more profitable.

3. Insight Management and Fear

If I were to write a book on fear, I would use a title such as "Welcome Fear!" to demonstrate that you never have to deny the existence of fear, because it's like the monster in the wardrobe. The deeper you bury yourself in the bedclothes denying it, the more it grows and terrorises you. So the magic phrase would be, "OK, fear, talk to me – I'm listening." And as you'd listen, your fear would become smaller, because once you listen to its warnings, it stops calling your attention.

Refusing to listen improves nothing. Taking account of what you're facing is vital for you to be able to respond/react in time and correctly. The opposite, to freeze, leads to financial and emotional death.

On other occasions what lies behind fear is paradoxically a more or less conscious desire. "I'm afraid you want to leave me" might also be, "I would like you to leave me because I'm incapable of taking the decision, and that's what I need." Identifying a projection and taking responsibility for the reality you generate is essential to happiness and gives you the feeling of being in control without the sensation of having a chip on your shoulder or being the world's victim.

Other confusions might be, "I'm afraid you're attacking me because in reality it's me who wants to attack you." I have special experience of this case because of a huge Dutch client who came to tell me that he lived in terror, certain that he was about to be mugged in the street at any moment. He could barely sleep at night, and when he managed to, he would suffer from terrible nightmares.

My own feeling in his presence was also one of fear, but it was very different, because what caused the fear was the man himself. He was racked with internal fury mixed with aggressive paranoia, which gave me the feeling that he really might attack me. This information was important, because it helped me get him to see that the attitude he projected in the streets was frightening for everybody else too. He was nearly seven feet tall, had tight spiky hair, dreadful tattoos, and sudden movements; to make it worse the heavy rock that burst from his earphones made communication with him impossible. You could see that inside, he really thought the world had it in for him but that in reality he was poised to attack, so that his greatest fear was actually of harming others if he lost control.

Fortunately he had enough self-awareness to realize something was wrong with his perception and that he couldn't manage it by himself. What triggered him to seek help was when, pushed by his father, he accepted a job as a night-time security officer. The job was performed alone and he felt even more frightened. Soon he was offered to carry a gun, skipping the mandatory psychological tests. At that point he was sensibly scared enough to resign. He sought my help, got better and recovered his sleep, peace and love.

This story describes the journey he made from darkness to light. In the darkness lay the reasons for being so frightened and which he couldn't understand (his size alone meant he could kill someone with just a blow, and they gave him a gun!). Having the courage to stop and face his fear, take ownership of his anger, meant that he was beginning to express and place limits on his life, that he was growing out of being the wounded and threatened child and becoming an adult, easing the pressure cooker of his life so as to live in peace. People who just repress it, run the risk of ending up like so many tragic cases we've heard about who explode one day and murder people senselessly in a supermarket or a school.

In many situations involving politics, business, the stockmarket and even more personal matters, this example of fear of one's own projected violence is a daily occurrence. The world teems with false rumours, manipulations, aggression, and the tension that must be borne to avoid preventive or responsive aggression. History shows us the example of how Nazism used the natural fear felt by its leader, which echoed throughout Germany, trembling behind sanctions of war to invade and expand with the excuse that this would prevent the invaded nations from invading Germany. It was insane, and the Holocaust was the greatest madness in history, but at the time the Germans didn't see it like that. They felt that, as victims, it was justified, and the Nazi party was even democratically elected. You have to bear in mind the fact that in conflict, the party that is the most aggressive always sees itself as the victim.

Hold. That's the key word when it comes to fear: whoever feels frightened should open their eyes wide and hold tight to the hammer to defend themselves, but hold it still, don't swing first. History is full of battles where neither side accepts starting it; they always think it was the other who made the first move. If you read versions of the same war according to historians from opposing countries, you will be amazed. Holding means not only holding back, but having the maturity to continue feeling emotion and perceiving reality and at the same time being able to not explode. You mustn't confuse holding with repressing, because repressive energy is against movement, it adds more tension and conflict.

However, what is more normal and humane is the initial reaction of triggering aggression and control mechanisms instead of accommodating the fear. This is much more understandable, and all the more so if the party reacting is the government of a recently attacked superpower, but this does not mean that greater control is more efficient, certainly not at the cost of such action and the prices we must all pay. Control is necessary, efficient and must be present when there is implied risk or threat. It's crucial to trust in institutions, authority and people and yet many actions where "control" is exercised reveal a false sense of control.

President Obama (June 19 2013) declared: "threats to freedom can arise from our own fears". From my point of view he took a huge step forward in a process of emotional maturation which his own nation has been in need of taking since it suffered the grotesque aggression of the Twin Towers. Realising that now is the moment to hold the fear without implementing fresh coercive freedom-focused measures is definitely a demonstration that you have done the work and a good example for us all to follow in our own small field of activity.

If you want energy to flow, you must resist raising barriers to its movement. You cannot ask your department to be more agile if at the same time, you are imposing supervision in the forms of checks and audits, etc. How would it be if every passenger wanted to perform their own blood alcohol level test on the pilot before take-off, just to be sure? You would never get off the ground. The line between control and mistrust is very fine and can be inadvertently crossed in a second. Control taken to the extreme is paranoid and highly dysfunctional. The thought police described by George Orwell in his brilliant novel *1984* not only put an end to creativity and innovation, but also to any hint of colour, life and light.

Let's take a look at the physiological side. Traditional Chinese medicine believes that there are five seasons, five elements, five main archetypical animals, etc. In winter, the dominant emotion is fear, and when listened to with wisdom it gives rise to an attitude of recognition, of not wasting energy, of not going out and of exploring inside. Metaphorically one flees from the threat of cold, as one could flee in a crisis from excessive pageantry expenses. Energy is focused by concentrating attention on what is here and now, rather than opening up new centres, projects, fires. Winter energy corresponds to the kidney – vitality and sexuality – as necessary for work as for getting the most out of life. If your fear stops provoking a prudent attitude and becomes an excessive or groundless emotion, it becomes sick and paranoid, sapping vital energy and enjoyment, both yours and your team's. The antidote to fear is humour. Play the monkey a bit (a powerful archetypical animal), get back your bodily movement, dance, laugh at yourself and relate to others, affectionately and physically. Enjoy. Your energy levels will rise again and your suspicions will fall to a healthy and reasonable level.

So fear and an absence of pleasure go hand-in-hand, interacting. If you aren't enjoying life, your energy will seep away and you'll find yourself afraid to launch yourself into life, achieve your desires and develop the projects you want to. Moreover, if you're scared, you'll cease to innovate, learn and experience the opportunities in life and you'll shrink back to what you already know. You must leave your comfort zone. Do things differently. Break away from inertia and routine, come back to life. What happens if one day, instead of scurrying home from work you decide to take a walk and enjoy the evening? What would happen if you had a beer with your colleagues? No doubt a number of people would say, "My husband/wife would kill me". Or would you say, "What? With all the jobs waiting for me at home?" or "Walk? I have a car – why would I want to walk?" If you take the chance to experience the new every day, you'll retain the feeling of being alive and the happiness to generate and defend new projects. If you stick with the known, you'll break the chain that generates hope and happiness, and sooner or later you'll lose your vitality and desire to do anything.

Some people say that it's better to develop your understanding of what you do know rather than attempt something new and risk finding nothing. As always, there are no universal rules, but the syndrome of "this has worked until now" becomes increasingly serious – paralysing with devastating consequences as shown by the number of bankruptcies in recent years. Come out of your comfort zone: live, create, innovate and enjoy it.

Another ancient tale recounts that in the Sufi tradition, a man named Nasrudin was looking for his keys under a street light. Assorted passers-by saw him and gave him a hand to find them, until at last, one of them asked him if he was sure he had lost them there. Nasrudin answered cuttingly that he had actually lost them in his house, but his "house" was very dark, while out in the street under the street lamp, it was very light. It seems absurd, but everyone does precisely the same thing. When you prefer to stay with what's comfortable you carry on, handcuffed to the past, to an image of what's no longer there. You have to look again without prejudice in order to see reality, discard what has crumbled to make space for the new.

There are two special cases that need to be tackled: fear of failure and fear of success. People who carry a lot of fear of failure move little, don't take chances and don't move outside their safety zone. They are also prone to leaving doors open, yet they don't walk through them. They neither throw anything away nor break anything in case they may need it. They are insecure creators, because when they find something they like they freeze and cease creative activity, fearing that anything they add will ruin what's been achieved up to that point. I can understand that attitude – it's very common. I recall my first experiences painting with oils, and when I liked something in my picture, I froze, unable to continue to develop it for fear of destroying it. However, he who wishes to become a great painter must have the nerve to risk the good and pretty in order to achieve the excellent and sublime.

On other occasions I have had clients with a less common type of fear: fear of success, sometimes concealed behind fear of failure or change. In this case there are sure to be psychoanalytical reasons (low self-esteem or childhood traumas) that weigh down the individual's journey to success. I recall one woman who told me she would prefer not to win a match because she wasn't sure how long she could keep on doing it. Another woman said she would rather dump her boyfriend before he dumped her, even though she saw no likelihood that he would ever do so. And yet another said that she could not bear the blame of being a professional success and eclipsing her husband who seemed to grow steadily less successful. There's also the case of a musician who never wanted to interpret the work of his dreams in the concert hall of his dreams because this would spell death – "nothing better could ever follow".

In conclusion, do not die of fear, or commit suicide, or freeze, or sleep your way through life with "eyelids as heavy as judgement day" (Bennedetti). If you're frightened, in addition to undertaking self-knowledge exercises to find out why you have this mechanism that leaves you isolated and cold, try to delve deeper into reality beyond what you think it is. Dare to live your life and let those who take part in it express themselves and respond. Shining light on your dark corners and crevices will prevent a lot of problems and facilitate a lot of success.

12
Create Your Own X-ray

1. Getting Ready to Start

At last the time has come to develop your own innovation x-ray by following the Innova 3DX Method. This step allows you to put everything you've worked on so far, individually, in order. It also shows you how you can acquire the overall perception needed to ensure that the innovative mechanism is fully operational.

This is a very simple process if you follow the instructions below step-by-step. In actual fact, for all those who are about to do this for the first time, I think I can say that you've reached the easiest part of all.

I just need to make one small but important clarification first. The Innova 3DX Method applications that are most in demand are as follows:

• Organization diagnosis: work that incorporates the evaluation of the company's three dimensions to identify the elements producing creativity leaks and those which by contrast, facilitate the process.

• Individual self-diagnosis: work focused on the internal strengths of a specific individual (second and third dimension), to identify individual brakes and strengths regarding the innovation and entrepreneurial process.

These are not, however, the only ones. Also required is an analysis with a systemic focus that deals, for example, with countries, regions or sectors.

Some adjustments will be needed as regards the dimensions and factors included in each analysis along with questions asked to perform each measurement. However, the methodology will be the same, so the guide shown below is valid for all – businesspeople, managers and entrepreneurs and also politicians, analysts, students, etc. Ready?

2. Construction Guide

2.1. Step 1: Building the Control Panels

To start with, take a look back and recover the measurements you already made of the dimensions and each of the factors. The first step is to enter the measurements in the control panels obtained so far.

Figure 12.1 Control Panel I (Innovative Ecosystem Panel)

Factors	Average obtained
Corporate culture	
Innovation culture	
Technological culture	
Work climate	
Physical framework	
Emotional framework	
Ethical and moral framework	
Spiritual framework	

Factors	Average obtained
Leadership and management style	
Resources	
Communication	
Autonomy	
Recognition and reward	

Figure 12.2 Control Panel II (Innovation Potential Panel)

Factors	Average obtained
Creativity	
Creativity self-assessment	
Technological profile	
Technological self-assessment	
Psychological profile	
Self-esteem	
Optimism	
Locus of control	
Orientation to learning	

Figure 12.3 Control Panel III (Passion for Innovation Panel)

Factors	Average obtained
Motivational expectancies	
Probability expectancies	
Value expectancies	
Fear of failure	
Orientation towards healthy fear	
Tolerance of failure	

This first step sums up all the measurements obtained in a single unit, which is a great help when proceeding with the subsequent analysis. Although many people think this is intuitive and needs no explanation, I'll show an example to prepare your own panel for the first time, just in case.

Let's suppose that the following responses have been obtained in the test on work climate, more specifically as regards the "physical space" pillar:

Figure 12.4 Measurement of Pillar 1 (Physical Space)

1.	The conditions of the physical environment I work in are good.	5
2.	The lighting is satisfactory.	6
3.	The temperature is satisfactory.	7
4.	The noise level is low.	7
5.	I am able to concentrate.	6
Average score		6,2

In that case, you would complete our panel as follows:

Figure 12.5 Control Panel – Example (I)

Work climate	
Physical framework	6,2

2.2. Step 2: Building the Diagnostic Panel

Having reached this point, and having focused your attention so far on data measurement and compilation tasks, let's move on to focus your activities on diagnosis, since the aim of this work is not to accumulate information, but to ensure that the information can be used to support decision-making.

The following step is to fill in the diagnosis panel.

Figure 12.6 Diagnosis Panel

Factors	Problem diagnosis
Creative ecosystem	
Corporate culture	
Work climate	
Management and leadership style	
Innovation potential	
Creativity	
Technological profile	
Psychological profile	
Passion for innovation	
Motivational expectancies	
Fear of failure	

To complete it, let's work with the following table of equivalencies:

Table 12.7 Table of Equivalencies

Score	Problem diagnostic and seriousness
0 – 3.5 (inclusive)	++ (very serious)
3.5 – 5 (inclusive)	+ serious
5– 6.5 (inclusive)	- (good state)
6.5 – 10 (inclusive)	- - (very good state)

How is it done? The direct equivalent shown by the table is entered into those factors that have only one element of measurement (creativity and technological self-efficacy). By contrast, in the case of those with more than one measurement element, the instruction is to enter the one with the lowest value.

Here's an example. Let's suppose that the following measurements were obtained in the second dimension:

Figure 12.8 Control Panel – Example (II)

Factors	Average obtained
Creativity	
Creative self-assessment	3,8
Technological profile	
Technological self-assessment	6,2
Psychological profile	
Self-esteem	10
Optimism	9
Locus of control	9
Orientation to learning	3

In the case of creativity and technological self-efficacy, the Control Panel directly provides the result that will be transferred to the equivalency table. However, in the case of the psychological profile, three very positive measurements have been obtained and one negative, so let's all take the lowest (orientation to learning - 3).

Hence, the panel will be completed as follows:

Figure 12.9 Example of the Diagnosis Panel (I)

Factors	Problem diagnosis
Innovative potential	.
Creativity	+
Technological profile	-
Psychological profile	++

Some people may wonder why they're not working with the averages again. The answer is simple: because you're seeking to identify and prioritise the problems (and hence their solutions). On the first panel you did it like this, because identification was done in the individual work of each explanatory chapter. If you did it like this, you'd leave behind a great many creativity leaks.

In actual fact, by following this approach the score for the psychological profile would be 7.75, a very positive score. However, as you can see, this is a factor that has problems indicating that actions are needed. This is obviously of no use to you.

2.3. Step 3: Building the Innovation X-Ray

You're now approaching the end, since this is the third and last step in the development of the x-ray. To build it, you only have to transfer the symbols from the diagnosis panel to the x-ray skeleton.

Below are the skeletons for those who made an organizational diagnosis as well as for those who focused on individual self-diagnosis.

Figure 12.10 Organizational Diagnosis

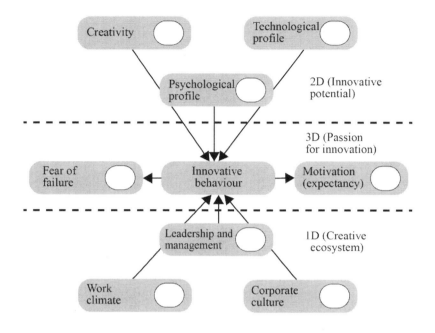

Figure 12.11 Individual Self-Diagnosis

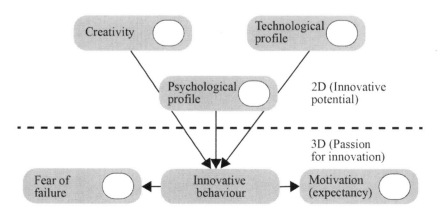

3. The Question and Answer Session

Now it's time for questions about the results shown for the x-ray plus the answers. These are some simple questions that will help you follow the analysis and discussion.

Are the three dimensions found in a good state? Are any of the problems associated with current innovative behaviour? Which ones? Is the environment causing a block? Is it human potential? Do you need a dose of passion? After this first analysis it's time to get down to the details, and with them, to locating the actual problems.

What are the elements that act as a spark – the strengths detected by the x-ray? Include here those factors for which the results could be: - - .

What are the elements that act as facilitators? Include here those factors for which the results could be: - .

What are the elements that act as brakes? Include here those factors for which the results could be: +.

What are the elements that act as blockers? Include here those factors for which the results could be: + +.

So now you know the sparks, strengths, brakes and blockers. So what do I do now? What should *we* do? Which direction do I take? Which direction do *we* take? How?

In order to set the innovative machinery running at full throttle, you have to denominate "a global balance" under the methodology, a scenario where all the factors score at least a – (absence of problems). The path to innovative leadership begins by achieving that status.

Special attention must be paid here to leadership and management style and the psychological profile, because if they reveal problems, those problems will directly hinder the process and sap the creative strength of the other factors from their respective dimensions. For example, pessimism can cancel a creative person's innovative strength.

So innovation is force, movement and action, yet the balance isn't sufficient. Sparks are needed to set off the process and accelerate it. This means that inno-leaders cannot accept this balance. They need to detect and stimulate their strengths and work on the construction of new ones because the path of innovation is a journey that involves overcoming problems and consequently, overcoming yourself without limits.

For the last question, "how?" – my recommendation is to begin at the beginning. Go back to reading the factors regarding which problems were detected in the x-ray, and consider your collective expertise in insight management and how it should be applied in this concrete case, here and now.

The Innova 3DX Method offers two additional tools to organizations that hope to lead in this field: benchmarking and influence quantification.

Benchmarking – comparative market assessment – offers a global perspective on the nature and origin of a problem, plus valuable information about the focus of the most effective solutions. To achieve this, it uses information obtained about thousands of professionals who've already taken part in this work.

For example, suppose you detect a high level of in-house pessimism, but benchmarking shows that the market is bursting with optimism? What will be your perception of the problem? You'd assume that something is not working well in-house and would work to find out what.

On the other hand, suppose that you also find pessimism very present externally and you are almost completely infected by it. To find an antidote you need to delve deeper into your understanding of its origin. In cases like this you'll almost always find both internal and external reasons. Unfortunately, when tackling a problem of global reach, deploying remedial actions runs into a tough challenge: what can be done to prevent yourselves from becoming re-infected when you emerge into the external world? Pessimism is contagious and contact with the external world is inevitable. Comparative assessment – benchmarking – won't provide solutions but it will provide the information needed to develop really effective corrective measures.

The Innova 3DX Method also offers quantification (and prediction) tools regarding influence and key performance indicators (KPI). This is especially useful for taking decisions about investment in remedial actions and for monitoring their effect over time.

Suppose that the x-ray reveals serious problems in three factors: corporate culture, work climate and leadership and management style? Where do you start? You could try throwing all your collective weight behind the problem, but resources are always limited, as is strength (and actions like this call for a great deal of energy). Why not prioritise? You could (and should) work on all three, but it would be more effective to put more weight on the factors that have the most influence on innovative behaviour, at least to start with.

This work should measure the influence of each factor, providing information like this:

Figure 12.12 Interpretation Example

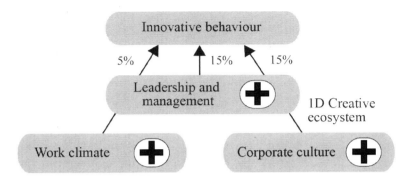

This would be interpreted as follows: the work climate is responsible for only five per cent of innovative behaviour, while leadership and management style and the corporate culture is responsible for 15 per cent.

In an environment of limited resources, would you invest the same effort, time and money in all three factors if all were serious? As the influence quantification shows, this wouldn't be the best path.

So now what? You've arrived at the end, but also at the beginning – the end of this diagnosis guide and the beginning of the journey to inno-leadership. There have been many questions, but also many answers and now you know where to begin and how to travel. From time to time obstacles may arise, but the effort is worth the trouble. It will produce valuable rewards.

13
The Importance of Sex

1. The Importance of Sex

I do wish such a brilliant title had been my idea, but unfortunately I can't claim it. I am, alas, forced to admit that I borrowed it from *The Economist,* the prestigious British publication that specialises in international relations and economy. The author used this phrase to title an article dealing with the fact that it is essential that female talent be rendered profitable. The article appeared in 2006, just before the beginning of the crisis, and it strove to alert its readers to the menace of the dangerous economic burden arising from the under-use of the female labour force.

The macroeconomic data that supports this phenomenon is devastating. The article reveals how the incorporation of women into the labour force has been, without a doubt, a major source of growth these last few decades. In real terms, this factor has meant an increase in gross domestic product (GDP) considerably in advance of the growth that took place in powerful technological giants and even countries such as China and India. When we add the work done in the home by women (domestic chores, elder- and childcare, etc.), without financial gain to women's contribution in the labour market, the figure exceeds 50% of the total GDP.

If we change our perspective and analyse forecasts of what the future holds for us, the figures are even more impressive. The real inclusion of female talent in the labour market would boost the USA GDP by a (not inconsiderable) 5%, a figure that rises to 9% for Japan, 12% for the United Arab Emirates, and peaks at 34% in Egypt.

And although much water has flowed under the bridge since the publication of this article, particularly in terms of a review as influential as this, nothing has changed, and the facts remain as current as ever. Right now women are the most powerful and promising growth engine we have available to us. And unfortunately, they remain one of the most under-used of resources.

According to International Labour Organisation (ILO) figures, in excess of 865 million women professionals are still being wasted today. Of these, 812 million live in emerging or developing countries. Can you imagine the impact their appearance in the business machine would have? And what sort of effect do you think it would have on the socio-economic development of their countries?

We shall never see a healthy society if women are doomed to suffer a labour market that denies them the opportunity to take part in it on grounds of gender. Nevertheless, this is just one of the reasons why urgent measures are needed. The low use of this 'resource', as it is known to economists, also happens to be a question of profitability, and for many, of plain survival.

What all this means is that governments must, as a matter of urgency, take remedial steps to lay the foundations for the structural transformation needed. Companies must also accept their share of responsibility, because unless they cooperate it will be impossible to solve a problem that emerged, is growing and continues to develop on their own doorsteps. But businesses are not alone. Each and every one of us can, and must, do our bit.

You may be wondering why. Why must we, too, accept this responsibility? Do we have yet another burden to bear? Don't we have enough? Surely, you think, this is really a problem to be solved by those holding the power: the politicians, the businessmen. If that's what you think, then you're wrong. It's their problem, is it? Yes, of course it is, and they ought to be well aware of it. It's a big problem for all of them, but it's also ours, because we're all, every one of us, responsible. It's a big problem for you, and it's a big problem for me, because if we don't start making use of women's potential and talent, we will cripple our own development and economic growth, and miss out on the very possibilities that this talent offers.

2. The Keys to Female Profitability

Let's take another look at the growth forecasts that factor women into the economic picture: 5% for the USA, 9% for Japan, 12% for the UAE, 34% for Egypt, etc. When you read figures as overwhelming as these, you are bound to find yourself wondering exactly what it is about the entry of women into the work force that would bring about these growth figures. What is it that changes with their presence? Why are they so profitable?

In the first place, naturally enough, we notice their effect on the human factor. We have all heard that as a general rule, women are very creative, great communicators and capable of remarkably effective team work. It has also been observed that when added to a mixed-sex team, that team's ability to solve an organization's problems increases. We all know how difficult it is to put our fingers on exactly what happens, but something certainly does, and what we do know is that men and women are different. This is a physiological reality and the capacity to effectively manage this difference could be significant and very valuable.

Secondly, we meet the economic arguments: recent research has revealed that women have a particular ability when it comes to making investments, something which in the medium- and long-terms will have a positive effect on the pockets of investors and shareholders. In a similar vein, a number of statistical studies have shown that companies with women on their boards of directors have better results than those that don't employ women. The OECD report, *Closing the Gender Gap: Act Now* (2012), highlighted the importance of a fresh viewpoint in the taking of strategic decisions. But the fact that these works, along with a great many others we could mention, have not received unanimous support should at least give us pause for thought.

However, there is a third fundamental reason which, in my opinion, overrides the others, and which every manager or entrepreneur should always keep to the fore: according to *The CIA World Factbook* (2013), the percentage of men in the world is 50.5%, compared with 49.5% women. But it is women who make 80% of all decisions regarding purchases. In other words, customers are almost always women. And yet business decisions doggedly leave them out of the picture. At first sight, this doesn't seem very sensible.

One example will suffice: of the 500 companies listed in the Standard and Poor's Index, less than 5% have female directors on their boards. If we break down the figures by sector, undertake a study by country, or change the size of the company, the numbers might fluctuate a little, but believe me, we would end up in the same place: hardly any women. What would you expect the outcome to be? Does anyone really believe that excluding women from the design, production, marketing and above all decision-making chain has no effect on it? Men and women think, feel and act differently. I certainly don't want to attempt to work out who is better and who is worse (nor do I believe I could), but what I do know is that it is *important* to accept, to understand and to handle these differences skilfully, and that means that women must be in the loop from the start.

In other words, if you are a member of a team that manages a business, if you are an entrepreneur, or if you are planning to launch a business venture, you must never forget one fact: female talent is one of the most valuable and under-used resources found in the marketplace. *Use it.* If, on the other hand, you happen to be one of those women trying to make her mark in the world and have found it very difficult, please, don't throw in the towel just yet. The future really is packed with fresh opportunities that we cannot ignore. This is our opportunity – and our responsibility.

I mustn't finish without making an important clarification to prevent mistaken interpretations about what I have just said. If anybody finds that they strongly disagree with the need to replace male talent with female talent, and with the profitability of doing so, they are right on the money except for one thing: I never mentioned any replacement of the kind, nor would I support it. I'm in favour of making the most of individual potential: 100%, men's *and* women's. Right now, when we are at last rediscovering the road to growth, there's room for everybody.

3. Insight Management and Gender

3.1. Before We Start to Talk About Gender in the Professional World: Free Yourself of Preconceived Ideas

The first thing I have to accept is that on this subject, more than any other, prejudice tends to get in the way of correct perceptions of reality. Also the way the same message changes, depending on if it's a woman or a man reading it to a man or a woman. The inertia that comes along with this kind of prejudice makes it look as though a great deal of aggression is mere defence, and that is a great pity. This is the reason why more than ever, I urge everybody reading this section of the book to start by taking deep breaths, empty your lungs, empty yourself of preconceived ideas and get rid of status quo ideas so that you can carry on building with the pieces of the puzzle that make up the more profound real truth, which is the one we create among all the others, starting from our own corner.

Having said this, I now risk prejudice by saying that it's me, Jorge, who is writing this part. The second thing I have to do is ask your pardon, since now that you're aware of the situation, you know that everything I write is filtered through me, a man, and well, you know what men are like etc. That's what we're like: prejudice precedes and sifts how we perceive reality, whether we like it or not. Indeed, the very fact that this part of the book starts with the mention of sex has already created a filter for some. Now you can carry on reading and breathing, emptying and filling yourself; you can read and work on your expectations since, like everything else in life, prejudice and reality are always very far apart.

3.2. Why a Sex-Focused Insight?

The reason for taking sex as our standpoint, or as it is more commonly referred to, gender, in a book like this has already been explained in macroeconomic terms, which is why I should like to concentrate on microeconomics, as 'micro' as the human mind itself, which when all is said and done is what is really hatching out at macro level.

I may be misjudging the historical moment, but the way I see it, there is no ruling gender, just as we should be championing the parallel development of left and right brain hemispheres, just as I insist that the more both sexes advance hand-in-hand, the better each can give of him or herself and add to the overall sum. This does not mean that there should be nobody at the rudder, so that the vessel is at the mercy of the waves, but it does mean that with appropriate humility, each of us will be able to accept that it may be better for the other to lead now.

Many people may claim that this is the century of woman, but I am aware of the dangers of preconceived leadership, and I suggest that we should steer clear of matriarchies and patriarchies as being nothing more than pendulum-like responses. In any case, I am for a world in which we all freely choose our space and, avoiding any prejudgement that this or that one is the best, that it's more masculine or more feminine. Those of us who can adopt this kind of thinking will be free to go where we will, without the oppression that arises from considering it to be related to this sex or the other. In other words, women will be able to operate in a world traditionally seen as masculine, and vice-versa. Society will always follow the acceptance of this, but what can we ask of society if, first of all, we have not accepted it within our own beings?

If removing our own prejudices from our deepest being is a complex business, then managing our own ego – step number two – is even more so; but it means that the historical moment has arrived when all individuals must look deep within themselves, must interrogate themselves, look squarely at their dark sides and take responsibility for the places they occupy in the world. Today more than ever, everything is possible. When we're willing to form a team with the other sex and continue sailing in the same direction, we complement and enrich ourselves, support and nourish ourselves, and are able to take on even greater projects. The key lies in the awareness and willingness to not carry on with the ancient sexist battle.

The focus on gender produces its greatest friction and fruits within the couple itself, whether this is on a personal or professional basis, both territories being the same in my case.

What I have appreciated, in my own realization, is that the comparison always exists, and that, as with yin and yang, one person will always see black or white "in comparison to". So even though you can achieve great things on the professional front, if the achievements of the person alongside you are even greater, it may seem as though your own are no big deal and vice-versa.

Working on one's essence, with the very nucleus of being, sends one back – sends me back – to a self-esteem not based on image or on narcissism. I am not my results because I am much more and yet much less. And, of course, I am not seen in comparison to, because I simply *am*. What I am sharing here is my experience, not my theory, and I am a firm believer in those who seek light within their lives, since when you reach a stage of knowing yourself where you can be empty of yourself with some degree of regularity, you can access the part that is both the most human and yet the most sublime part of being; the space where you can be both a person, at your ease, and also a superman or superwoman, a combination of humility and stardust.

Historically women have had little opportunity to flourish in many fields, there have been some who learned to shine discreetly so that society and even their own partners wouldn't mind, but this was a complex, often thankless, task, which on occasion led to suicide. If we take a glance at the cases of Camille Claudel and Rodin, or Marie and Pierre Curie, for example, we see as much light as darkness, paradoxically, since in a firmament of such brilliant stars we would tend to expect only to be dazzled.

Curie is an example of the newcomer to the world of the Nobel prize – twice! – in that while she was an absolutely brilliant scientist, she published much less than her husband because it was understood that she should focus on the family, and the time she spent on her work caused her to feel tremendously guilty, because it was time not focused on home. This is the way such ideas which had been built into the female psyche would operate, ideas that men of the time never had, and clearly it's better to start by expelling such concepts before deciding later which ones you can live with and which you can't.

An accusing finger has for a long time now been pointed at men, as a group, or at least at a male-focused society, as the source of all the ills of so many women. Personally I find this attitude of little value, since rarely any society does feel guilty of any accusation, and still fewer react because of it. I therefore feel that it is crucial to shift the focus from the societal to the personal. In fact, responsibility always falls upon the individual, of either sex (may this help recovering some belief in political systems and parties, given that they only exist as a sum of many individuals).

3.3. Gender Competition

For centuries, the demarcations between the spheres of each gender's actions were very clear: for woman, it was the home, while for a man, it lay outside of the home – in hunting mammoth, bear or fish, or making war. When women made their appearance in the labour market a lot of positive things happened. Women were no longer absolutely dependent on men's income and men could now look forward to some economic support from women.

Not everything was positive, as I insistently claim from the insight management angle, resistance to change results in egos flourishing like naked swords.

Men are afraid of losing control and power, and as we have already seen, the other face of fear is aggression, which makes for sad but common news; women nursed a traditional resentment in the face of serious injustices they were not even permitted to mention. Now, of course, they can, and so much pain can easily turn to rage. Much of today's gender-related violence is, in my opinion, the result of wounds which I hope can now stop happening and heal speedily. To that aim, I encourage us all to communicate, listen, and to raise the standards of our value system.

It also turns out that not only both parties compete now in the same areas but also, they no longer fight together for a common interest; this is the cause and effect of differentiation – of not belonging, of clinging to the power of one party by boosting individuality in place of unity, and so on. Many divorces are a blessing for all the family, but just as many reflect the consumerist and whimsical behaviour of an individual, which leaves whole families in shock.

The cinema is often a source of images and experiences which, if viewed with an awareness that goes beyond mere entertainment, can teach us a great deal. Examples would be *The Method* in the professional area, and *Samsara* in a more spiritual field, both films which seek to show how women choose family and motherhood, while men may drift back to pursuing the male goal: freedom. What I would like to mention here as a factor in the field of technology is the Athena phenomenon, which works with greater or lesser punch in so many other areas where enduring in your work at a certain age implies, giving up on family intimacy, child-rearing, completing domestic chores, etc.

If we can set aside our prejudices, we see that everything is valid and that we all contribute what we can and wish to. But if we force the machinery by means of erratic impulses associated with images of success that are dissociated from our authentic inner lives (such as being an engineer like Dad or a housewife like Mum), we are in real danger, since we are genuinely risking our lifetimes pursuing careers or families that in reality do not connect with who we really are. In other words, freedom and easier access to the labour market for women nowadays means they can now decide whether it is more important to seek a top managerial position and put motherhood off until later. However, the moment comes and goes without leaving an opportunity for motherhood, which must be recognized as an actual factor in corporate social responsibility.

Awareness renders each and every one of us free to choose our pathway – and it is this that I aim for with everybody who comes to consult with me on an individual basis. This means that some men choose to be househusbands and some women opt for management, and when they do so from a healthy, knowing and responsible awareness these are both excellent options. The problem is that these are very deep waters, and such a degree of awareness is not easy when urged by consumerism, information saturation and social pressure.

In other words, while there is no doubt that most men see the home as a comfortable place where they feel secure and supported, that same majority may also seek freedom as the place where they wish to perform and record their actions, to see who they are through professional and personal conquests. In the case of women, even if she wants to compete with a man, and succeeds in defeating him, she comes to experience an existential vacuum. This crisis, when well-focused, can be an opportunity for growth – through her own femininity, through closeness with the women of the tribe, the company, the family or the social gathering, whatever it may be. I want to take this opportunity to say that working groups, be they male or female, are certainly the best place for finding yourself. In that space where the eyes of the other sex are absent, you can honestly and intimately see yourself for the first time, see your same-sex brothers or sisters become more healthy and transcend what has not been possible to transcend for generations.

3.4. Power and Psychopathy from the Point of View of Gender

Throughout history a great many of our leaders have been men and also serious psychopaths. This may seem like a slightly shocking statement, but if you pause for a moment to give some thought to psychopathic behaviour, you will see that it is not so far from the truth.

The first thing you notice is that the psychopathic/narcissistic personality possesses great magnetism, which means that people possessed of it tend to be very charismatic, tend to win elections, to lead armies or multinationals – and/or indeed, sports teams – with merciless and military force, with efficiency as far as the goal is concerned, and indifferent as to methods and/or collateral damage. If you think about it for a moment, you realize that this is the way it has to be; that in war you want a leader who helps you win, not one who is kind to the enemy. Of all the international conflicts I have studied, I have only found one exception: that of Tibet, a great model of spiritual development. Tibet managed to avoid becoming psychopathic in its struggle with China and forging ahead at any price (although since they lacked any possibility of responding proportionately, any such attitude would have been ridiculous). On the matter of psychopathy, neurologist James Fallon found that in thousands of magnetic resonance images of individuals with psychopathic characters, including his own, there was one common component: their brains lacked any activity in the frontal and temporal lobe areas, the regions responsible for empathy and self-control. This would explain their moral lack of capacity or ability to control their impulses, but the regions responsible for stress and emotion also appeared to be inactive, closing the circle on the insensitive personality. According to Fallon, people with this genetic tendency have within their character a trigger that can make them behave dangerously, for society, or simply render them extremely powerful. There is no doubt that the child-soldiers we see so many of in Africa, capable of single-handedly exterminating an entire village, reach this stage by overexposure to violence, and so there will be genetically similar cases of those who, if raised in a good environment, one that is stable and protective, will never turn to violence (as is the case with this particular scientist).

Therefore, whenever there is a threat of absorption by another country, company and so on, certain aspects of psychopathic behaviour of the most warlike (what Aristotle called Phylakes) are often welcome, but it must be contained by the equally Aristotelian sages, the Archontes. Unfortunately, the historical reality of humanity is as far from Aristotle as it is from Plato's world of ideas, revealing a glaring absence of containment and morality in the construction of systems, international trade rules, justice and social development, etc. In power, there is a serious shortage of enlightened sages, or at least it would appear that they soon give in to the corruptions of power. Like Saint Philip Neri, the man to whom the Pope offered a cardinalship, only to have it rejected because, "I prefer paradise," I, too, strive to stay out of the eye of the storm, praying that those who do dare to sail in these waters manage not to drown the lot of us.

On the domestic front, it has been the woman who has traditionally brought light, sensitivity and nourishment to the home, acting as an absolutely essential mechanism for the survival of the race, village, tribe, etc. Nevertheless, as with any psychopathic tendency, the overexposure of these women to hostile environments produced and produces women who are just as psychopathic, whether they end up as terrorists or leaders of international organizations, multinationals, or even an NGO. As mentioned before, the disguise they wear is irrelevant; what matters is their level of awareness, which as we have explained with regard to magnetic resonances, if not practised, tends to disappear, even physiologically.

We can now observe many senior female managers who are just as aggressive or even more so, than their male counterparts, who act with cruelty and a lack of empathy. Often these women have turned into the worst enemies of the feminine and women. An obvious example is the large number of woman-on-woman sexual harassment cases, where reconciliation is sought. Instead of offering support, they seem to say, "if I don't need it, then nobody does," as if they are immune to their own injuries as well as to those of others, like psychopaths.

However, if you thought that all is lost because the world is in the hands of psychopaths, you would be wrong. Other studies using magnetic resonance, this time on people who practise meditation, show that such practices allow for the activation of all the areas of the brain, generating synaptic connections, new networks of knowledge and understanding. It also proves that meditation reduces the rate of cellular destruction and even stimulates the generation of cells that in the past were thought could no longer be generated in an adult brain.

This is why I continually emphasise working with meditation, the place where you not only rest but manage to harvest fruit from the fertile vacuum – ideas, inventions, fluidity in thinking or perspective for conflict resolution. Thanks to these practices we can become better people and generate better environments for work, relationships, the family, the company, the tribe and the state. This is one of the great journeys of humanity for our time: to humbly go back and empty ourselves of ourselves, open our hearts and accept our own and others' limitations; understand that processes take their own time and that not all ideas and impulses should be carried out, psychopathically. Some should be contained out of simple respect for ourselves, our fellow human beings and future generations.

3.5. The Image of Power and Sexual Capital: the Capacity to Influence

When we observe the anthropological rites of many cultures, we see that an individual's image is always connected to their process of empowerment for accomplishing some task or another, very unlike the common empty usage of image that we are accustomed to nowadays.

While Native Americans painted their bodies and faces for battle, the Lisbeth Salander character from the well-known film saga, "Millenium", presents herself appropriately, according to her own lights, with the perfect punk hairdo, boots, black leather, studs, white face makeup, etc. This is her way of preparing for battle just as a Cherokee warrior would. It is obvious that Lisbeth Salander's image in this case is not designed to seduce the court, but to stand up to her enemies, feeling empowered. Adapting your aspect to suit the environment can be a way of reaching others, but not at the price of losing your personal power.

The question I ask now, from the sex/gender angle is this: why must the professional woman be rendered masculine? Each individual should have the freedom to proceed in a manner that locates his or her echo, that locates his or her own power and strength. Good girls who dress the way they are expected to dress will become no more than a reflection of what we hope they may be, and will be so well camouflaged that no one will remember them. Those who dare to be themselves, however, including playing with their own image, may well be criticised but they will also be praised and remembered, and will shine with their own light.

From this point of view, men have much less leeway as regards appearances. The tribes of the American West painted themselves, while now women do, whereas we cannot. It's a matter of culture. The other day I ran into a group of Scots in a German airport travelling to support their football team, and they were proudly wearing kilts. It's fairly obvious that in the occupational area there is very little wiggle room, although some does exist. When my father began working as an engineer he would never have gone to the office without a tie, not even for a single day, but nowadays many managers, parliamentarians and even ministers do, and nothing happens.

On the sexual capital front it is clear that nobody should abandon any aspect of their power in any of the ways it manifests, women most of all. Individual power is observable everywhere, from the natural world of insects and animals, to us human beings. Likewise, it is also expressed in the beautiful colours of bird or insect plumage that can be used to trap victims, fascinate and seduce, appear imposing and sometimes, to mimic others, another seductive ploy. Eventually we may just thus revel in the glory of the divine nature each of us possesses and our plumage announces that. This goes without saying for some, though that's not the case for others. Prejudicial comments are still rampant, uttered by men and women alike, proving that they create the problems, not the individual who is comfortable in his or her own body. Should a jellyfish hide its shape and colour because some sea bather finds it ugly? Watch out for the sting …

As with everything I say, this is true in part – the heads and tails of all coins are like this, so I always insist that it is still important to respect the culture of a place or a company, since in some cases, a flamboyant or attention-grabbing outfit might cause authentic shock, which would be neither productive nor desirable, and if a culture and/or a country are out of line you could be buying problems.

Since this part of the book addresses sex, let's not sidestep homosexuality, a thorny subject with no place for prejudice. On this subject, a large majority of the populace have yet to adopt a healthy attitude. For some strange reason, it seems easier to accept the image of a seductive heartbreaker predator than the concept of a male or female homosexual. To me it is difficult to understand that the former even provokes admiration while homosexual people still seem to make many uncomfortable: "Well, if she's a lesbian, it's best if I just treat her as a man," (a mistake, since there are also extremely feminine lesbians), or the masculine version, "I always thought he was so masculine," (open your eyes, he could be packing more testosterone than you). Other versions could be, "If he's gay, he might fancy me, and that could be awkward," (and it could also happen if the other party is also heterosexual. So what's bothering you? Is this a real threat? Take it easy …).

Homosexuality has been and continues to be some kind of bête noire as far as society is concerned. This attitude became so entrenched that historically speaking, many countries as civilised as England and Belgium had laws against it. Some cases became sadly notorious, such as those involving Oscar Wilde and the poets Rimbaud and Verlaine who were artists of enormous creativity and significance in their field. This is not the kind of people you can afford to do without!

We now know that there are so many homosexuals at all levels of society that my advice to anyone with any prejudices in this area is that they should start dealing with them immediately, as, indeed, they should with any similar prejudices regarding gender, race or anything else. People are people, and all have something unique to offer for those who know how to value them beyond their own limitations.

Not long ago I found myself reading a letter which Einstein was supposed to have written to his daughter, in which he confessed that the greatest transformative power in existence was love. I fully share this view: individuals who are deprived of their own way of loving become timid and toxic, and we find ourselves avoiding them. But if we can set aside our prejudices and simply allow ourselves and everybody else to *be* without imposing a particular pattern, we would find that we are enabling this transformative energy to produce an infinity of quantum leaps of every kind.

14
Female Digital Depopulation

1. The Digital Case

These days innovation is a digital matter. By now it should be obvious to all that both the most ground-breaking innovations and the tiniest improvements in our daily lives almost always come about thanks to new technologies. For this reason, and because the experts in the European Commission claim that if we can attain a 50% labour division in the new technologies sector, the European GDP should grow by some €9 billion, we shall concentrate our attention here on the position occupied by women in this promising labour market which includes both technological and digital profiles. On this basis I urge all readers to perform their own investigations within the activity sectors that most concern them. You will see how and why you should work to boost the rate at which women are hired in this area.

For every job that disappears from the traditional world, nearly three jobs are created in the digital environment. In ground-breaking areas like big data, it is estimated that 4.4 million new jobs will have been created by the year 2020 globally. In the same vein, official forecasts state that in the next four years, within the European Union five million jobs will be generated in the field of developing new mobile apps, which will bring with it a growth figure of some €63 billion. These are just some of the examples of the occupational revolution taking place within a sector that has not only not been dragged down by the grinding crisis we have been forced to live through, but to the contrary, this revolution has established its workers as being among the most in demand and best paid in the world.

In contrast with these optimistic figures, we find that in the specific case of the European Union, of every 1,000 women now graduating university, only 29 are skilled in new technologies, versus 95 men. This means that of the total of all professionals who make up the initial pool, only 23% will be female. If we explore the digital gap still further, the figures reveal that by the time they reach age 30, only 20% of these women will still be working in the sector in which they intended to specialise. To put it another way, 80% of the 23% of the women aiming for a career in this sector will already have abandoned it. And as if that were not enough, if the rules of the game remain the same, a further brain drain will then take place such that by age 45, only 9% will still be in the profession.

So what does all this mean? Female depopulation in this sector has become one of the key engines behind the growing "digital gap" which is very concerning to governments. For those unfamiliar with the term, this is the name given to the mismatch between professional supply and demand in this most promising of labour markets. For example, official sources warn us that by the year 2020, the US will be finding it all but impossible to locate 1.4 million of the total ICT (information and communications technology) professionals it will need. And yet only 12% of the professionals who set out to study these subjects are women.

In the specific case of the European Union, the official figures are also available for all to study. Experts foresee a shortfall of between 505,000 and 864,000 positions by the end of the year. Faced with figures like these, does anybody still fail to see the need for action? Women and children must not let this opportunity slip.

2. The Bonfire of False Beliefs

It is a truth universally acknowledged: we have a serious problem when it comes to social and cultural stereotypes. Too many people have always thought (and continue to think) that technology is not for women, that this is the man's area. There has also never been any shortage of people convinced that women don't like technology, that it doesn't suit them. Indeed, women themselves have often thought that they were less well skilled than their male companions in making use of it, and that they had less technological effectiveness despite the want of any grounds for thinking so.

We also note a general belief, a myth, that this profession is a *man's* thing. We women like to spend our time in relationships with others, and the idea of sitting in front of a computer screen for hours on end isn't sexy enough. And we also find that women with "family responsibilities" (I am deliberately using inverted commas …), or those who seek them believe that this kind of job is not compatible with reconciliation problems (long days, night work and so forth). Those are problems that can only be solved by a very balanced domestic situation and often in company with outside help, which is not always available.

But supposing we were to follow the same train of thought with regard to the medical profession or journalism – would we reach the same conclusion? Do those women who plump for medicine, just as an example, find themselves racked by doubts when they think of the long shifts they may have to work when it falls to them?

Let's go a little further and consider the case of women who opt for journalism. Is their everyday life a matter of little importance to them? Do they give it a second thought? Probably many do, but when it comes to thé question of vocation, the final decision has almost always been taken right from the start.

So what's the difference when it comes to technology? The answer is obvious: we have a tough problem caused by stereotypes and false beliefs (whether social, cultural, concerned with the nature of the profession, etc.) which results in the fact that ever since they were little girls, women felt no attraction to this kind of work.

Where did it all start? I'm betting that a lot of people know the answer to that already.

Does anybody remember this advertisement? This is just one example which I will use in our little investigation. If you want to go into the subject in rather greater depth, I'm sure that you'll easily find hundreds of similar examples that will lead you to the same conclusions.

Questions:

1. Why do you work your modem with only one hand?

2. Can a modem be sexy?

3. How would you feel if all the new technology professionals in the world wore that uniform?

4. Do you think that the aim is to get a man or a woman to buy the modem?

Those of you who bothered to perform this exercise should now take a few more minutes to consider this historical example. This is not a waste of time, right?

So where am I headed with all this? The fact is that the creation of the stereotypes and false beliefs that currently keep women out of this sector is the work of a stream of marketing campaigns and the efforts of the communications media. But nowadays examples are much more difficult to find. With rare exceptions they are a thing of the past, and yet despite this, our thinking and beliefs have stayed rooted to those times, and we really need to change them once and for all. We can't let ourselves be held back by them. Let's build a bonfire and burn the lot.

So far, we have concentrated on the fact that women have been excluded from the world of the technological professional, but we shouldn't forget that this is not the only problem facing us; this is just a part of it. We have to make every effort we can to ensure that the foundations are laid for systems that will encourage the inclusion of women in this area, but we also have to create mechanisms that stop them from dropping out after a few years. In short, we have to work to ensure that the "Athena factor" starts to disappear.

For those of you unfamiliar with this name, it has become one of the most common ways of referring to the phenomenon whereby women abandon a profession in the field of the sciences, engineering and technology. It was coined in a *Harvard Business Review* article in 2008 that was both controversial and widely discussed: "The Athena Factor: Reversing the Brain Drain in Science, Engineering and Technology." The article revealed the conclusions of an interesting piece of research designed to explain why women who launched their careers in those fields sooner or later decided to change course.

The published figures left no room for doubt. The research showed that globally, 41% of the people who began their professional adventure in these three areas were women. And alas, according to the statistics, at some point during their careers, 52% of them decided to abandon them. The inevitable question is: why?

Many people will assume that there are reasons that don't need a great deal of explanation; that can be lumped under the label of motherhood. We have certainly all heard that explanation before. Yet I feel that on the grounds of my extensive experience in the field, I shall have to ask whether that is the real reason those women decided to dump their careers. In fact, I suspect that it is an excuse; nothing more than a final nudge that caused women to jump in a direction that they had been thinking about already for a long time.

Allow me a moment or two to explain the two forces that normally line up to explain the genesis of this problem, together with my personal take on them.

3. Corporate Culture

We now possess a great deal of evidence, plus field studies, which show that female talent is all too frequently misread and goes unacknowledged in the world of business. We have surely all read or heard some story like that.

I would like to add one further consideration to this fairly general thought: is it only female talent that is not recognized? Could it be merely the tip of a much larger iceberg? It is possible that a very large number of companies – or rather, their management – find it difficult to recognize anything which is different from their usual pattern? And that doesn't just mean recognizing it, but also managing it.

Let's take a look at the problem from another angle. Is there a positive side? I say that because there almost always is, and in this case, twice over.

When we find ourselves faced with a situation resistant to the idea of taking on new talent, which would bring fresh ideas and viewpoints, we become tougher and stronger and find ourselves having to sharpen our wits to unsuspected levels, and as far as innovation is concerned, this is distinctly useful. This becomes a shared problem. It is a problem for the women launching their careers in businesses unaccustomed to them, and it is also a problem for the men who are called upon to stand out from the rest and shine in environments where there is low tolerance for change. More often than not, these environments are ruled by a fear of doing things differently – simply because they have survived as they are so far, because things have worked.

But that's not the whole story. In my experience, when a certain moment comes in which worth has been demonstrated, when entry barriers have been overcome, progress is (usually) much easier. If we are willing to risk standing out from the crowd (or have no other option) and are initially successful, and make sure this is noticed, the rest is much easier.

So, is the culture really the force that leads to the career abandonment scenario? It certainly is; there is no doubt that this is the case, and it is a very powerful force, but … what if we see it as a test of toughness for everybody who decides to take advantage of what it is that differentiates them from others, which makes them profitable?

4. Loneliness

We women are alone, we feel alone, there are no female reference points and so few female companions. This is a powerful feedback loop. And almost always, it is loneliness that stands out as one of the most conclusive factors in deciding to abandon a professional career in the world of technology.

Is there anything we can do? In the short term there would seem to be no way out. So why not change the chip?

My professional career started nearly twenty years ago, and since then I have always been surrounded by men in my work. It has always been like this, without exceptions. This is something I have encountered in both business and academia, and it has always been there. I would have loved to have seen more women in my environment, but that wasn't the case. It wasn't their decision. Given their absence, I made efforts to create an environment where they were more present, at least as travelling companions.

This being the case, I have no difficulty in admitting that I got where I am today thanks to the unconditional support I received from many of those men who surrounded me. I never felt alone as a woman, because I decided to forget gender and concentrate on people. Naturally, as life has progressed I have met some extraordinary men who have supported me without ever expecting anything in return, but there have also been many who have not been exactly what you could call amiable, because they never would have chosen to work with me. Should I have allowed myself to be weighed down by that kind of burden? Their burden? It was too much work and I had too many other things to do.

I find that I can't end this section without taking a few lines to acknowledge the women who have worked with me. I have met a great many extremely intelligent women, women who were courageous fighters, too, but there were also many who did not make things easy. Why? I have given a great deal of thought to the question, entertained many possibilities, but failed to come up with an answer that I'm completely happy with – one that leaves me the certainty of being right. Fear? Jealousy? Competition? Insecurity? I don't know. So I content myself with one last thought on this thorny problem: we have to learn to support each other. We cannot be our own worst enemies. If we keep on like that, without backing each other, then in my humble personal opinion, the feeling of loneliness may not be so bad a choice.

So let's all just entertain some awareness and responsibility regarding this problem. We need female talent so that our businesses can innovate, and, of course, to do away with the digital gap that in this sector appears more glaring each day. If we all take this first step and do our own little bit whenever we get the chance, the lack of women in this area will be history.

Conclusion

If you glance back you'll see what a long road we've travelled together. All this time you've kept in mind the important role that is now played by innovation in the development of a country and its business fabric. A clear example is the experience of economies such as Israel, New Zealand and Chile, where innovation has become established as an obvious lever for growth. The same thing is happening in markets and in individuals, because the micro is projected onto the macro and vice versa: innovation and business success travel hand-in-hand.

The evidence that bears it out leaves no room for doubt, and the result is that every day more and more businesses decide to integrate innovation as a central feature of their competitive strategy. For all, the theory is very simple: unleash innovation. The way it's done, however, is the factor that gives rise to debate. How is it done? By improving the climate? Changing the culture? Rewarding the brave? Encouraging creativity? Through new technology projects? With new motivational strategies? Again, how?

The answer is simple: you must manage your intellectual capital and creative energy efficiently. This is nothing new. It means applying the same efficiency as in all other in-house and external processes. Some of these will certainly have reached a stage of excellence. So how can there be a justification for an exception? Why is intellectual and creative capital not being efficiently managed? Why are there still creativity leaks? Why is it that innovative energy is still failing to flow? There is no justification. But there is one explanation: the want of tools and know-how.

It is exactly this that turns this work into a unique tool. The Innova 3DX Method and the insight management that accompanies it allow for the deployment of mechanisms needed to manage innovative behaviour with efficiency. To achieve this, it explains how to monitor the three dimensions that generate creative energy or, alternately, that stall it: the creative ecosystem, innovative potential and passion. Thanks to its theoretical/practical explanations, the simplified assessment and self-assessment tests and the analyses and case studies from insight management – anyone interested in leading in this field will now have all the tools they need to liberate 100 per cent of their and their teams' capacity.

By using the formula provided by *The Passion Factor*, it becomes possible to accelerate the operations of the three engines that generate creative energy and manifests desired innovations.

More specifically, the techniques and recommendations incorporated into the first dimension favour the generation of vital individual and collective energy needed to make new things, and also to maintain it during day-to-day activities. Good management of this dimension accelerates the mechanism which acts from three driver foci: organization (acting externally), the mind and the body (in both cases where energy is extracted out). Good relationships with these three foci are the basis for overcoming oneself and expanding one's own limits.

The techniques and recommendations included in the second dimension stimulate the generation of mental energy, its focus and how to correctly channel it towards the production of new ideas and render them profitable. It stimulates both hemispheres of the brain and also the connections between them. It helps you to achieve maximum intellectual productivity, stimulating analysis and logic and fundamental thought mechanisms for competitive intelligence. At the same time, it makes it possible to detect the existence of self-imposed limitations that prevent creative contributions from emerging, and this is where the greatest enemies of mental clarity are born, along with convergent and divergent thought.

The techniques and recommendations included in the third dimension stimulate the generation of emotional energy capable of motivating and mobilising vital mental energy towards a common goal. At times it succeeds in arousing passion. It brings drive, direction and strength as part of the process of individual and collective creative empowerment demanded by this new era.

For all those in favour of inno-leadership, capitalization of diversity will be crucial, as differences make us more valuable. Homogeneity should never be our aspiration.

In our personal and professional life, all of us will experience stages that are easier and more difficult – good and bad playing cards, valleys and mountains. This book addresses creativity and passion not only from the point of view of the current demand for innovation, but also as a lifestyle. The insight management it includes is an eclectic method that comprises many disciplines to help the reader to see, understand and become empowered – and all of them are keys to innovation.

You can and you must govern your life with passion. Make choices, travel, with optimism and confidence in your own resources and those of the people with whom you bond. When you move, steering your craft in one direction or another, be aware of it. It will help you to know where you really are and whether you wish to advance, return or change course.

We offer three recommendations for this journey:

• Be humble. As Zen says: Do not look for masters but find them. Learn from your travelling companions, those closest to you, personally and professionally, such as your partner, parents, children, boss or subordinates. With the right attitude you can learn from everyone, even from someone foolish like Nasrudin, the idiot-savant whose Sufi tales we cited earlier.

- Move with freedom, happiness and without restrictions. Don't judge yourself. *Thought is much smaller than reality.* In fact, sometimes it has no connection with it, and when it does, it only hints at some small glimpse. Our perception of reality grows or should grow as we go on living, as we go on travelling.

- While you travel, laugh – laugh hard and often, and enjoy the experience because, if you don't, you won't be able to stand the journey. You'll become exhausted and won't be able to see more than a couple of steps ahead of you. If you laugh, the journey will be lighter and more pleasant; your eyes will be caught by other happy eyes like yours. And what's more, if you laugh you'll breathe deeply and won't have to weep to get your breath back.

Finally, we invite you to take part in an experiment: close your eyes and try to make your mind go blank. Breathe deeply and with awareness of what you're doing. Try to empty your mind and when thoughts arise, don't attach any importance to them, simply turn your attention back to your breathing. Wait a while, look, breathe again and look again. If some creative idea or image comes to you, throw yourself into it, set your creativity free with the passion of someone who knows they won't live forever, who's making the most of every second.

If nothing comes, nothing happens, then don't jump. Draw your bow and wait. It will come. Be confident. The ability to emerge strengthened from every crisis is in your hands. Companies and entrepreneurs with imagination, awareness and passion who decide to raise the inno-leadership banner will be the leaders of tomorrow.

Notes

Chapter 1

1   http://top100innovators.stateofinnovation.thomsonreuters.com/
2   https://www.fastcompany.com/3056427/most-innovative-companies/the-most-innovative-companies-of-2016
3   http://www.forbes.com/innovative-companies/

Chapter 4

1   http://www.who.int/features/factfiles/mental_health

Chapter 13

1   http://www.economist.com/node/6800723
2   http://www.oecd.org/gender/closingthegap.htm
3   https://www.cia.gov/library/publications/the-world-factbook/geos/xx.html

Bibliography

Chapter 1

EUROPEAN COMMISSION, Institute for Prospective Technological Studies (2015), EU R&D Scoreboard: *The 2015 EU Industrial R&D Investment Scoreboard,* Seville.

EUROPEAN COMMISSION (2016), Innovation Union Scoreboard, Brussels.

CORNELL UNIVERSITY, INSEAD and WIPO (2016), Global Innovation Index 2016: https://www.globalinnovationindex.org/, access 6 September 2016

Organisation for Economic Co-operation and Development, OCDE (2005), Manual de Oslo (online), http://www.oecd.org/sti/inno/oslomanualguidelinesforcollectingandinterpretinginnovationdata3rdedition.htm, access 6 September 2016

Chapter 2

HAMEL, G. (2007), *The Future of Management,* Boston, Harvard Business Review Press.

PETERS, T. J. and AUSTIN, N. (1985), *A Passion of Excellence,* New York, Random House.

RICARDO, D. (1817), *On the Principles of Political Economy and Taxation,* London, John Murray.

SCHUMPETER, J. A. (1939), *Business Cycles,* New York, McGraw-Hill.

SMITH, A. (1776), *An Enquiry into the Nature and Causes of the Wealth of Nations*, Edinburgh, Black.

TOWERS PERRIN and GANG and GANG RESEARCH (2003), *Working Today: Exploring Employees' Emotional Connections to their Jobs,* New York, Towers Perrin.

Chapter 3

PETERS, T. J. and WATERMAN, R. H. (1984), *In Search of Excellence: Lessons from America's Best-Run Companies,* New York, Harper & Row Publishers.

Chapter 4

AMERICAN PSYCHIATRIC ASSOCIATION (2000), *Diagnostic and Statistical Manual of Mental Disorders,* Washington D. C.

GOLEMAN, D. (1996), *Emotional Intelligence,* London, Bloomsbury Publishing.

LITWIN, G. H. and STRINGER, R. A. (1968), *Motivation and Organizational Climate,* Boston, Harvard University.

INTERNATIONAL LABOUR ORGANIZATION (2010), *List of Occupational Diseases of the OIT,* Geneva.

ROBBINS, S. P. (2005), *Administración,* Naucalpan de Juárez, México, Pearson Education.

Chapter 5

BIRDWHISTELL, R. (1970), *Kinesics and Context,* Philadelphia, University of Pennsylvania Press.

DECI, E. L. and RYAN, R. M. (1985), *Intrinsic Motivation and Self-determination in Human behavior,* New York, Plenum.

MEHRABIAN, A. (1972), *Nonverbal communication,* Chicago, Aldine-Atherton.

UNESCO (2009), Diversity and Performance Report, Paris.

Chapter 6

BRENOT P., (2007), Le Génie et la Folie, Paris, Odile Jacob.

BUZAN, T with BUZAN, B (1996) The mind map book: how to use radiant thinking to maximize your brain's untapped potential, Plume Books

DE BONO, E. (1985), *Six Thinking Hats: An Essential Approach to Business Management,* London, Key Porter Books Ltd.FREUD, S. (1930), "Civilization and its Discontents", from *Complete Works, XXI,* Buenos Aires, Amorrortu.

GUILFORD, J. P. (1985), "The Structure-of-Intellect Model", in Wolman, B. B. (ed.), *Handbook of Intelligence: Theories, Measurements, and Applications,* New York, Wiley: 225-266.

HUARTE DE SAN JUAN, J. (1991), *Examen de ingenios para las ciencias,* Madrid, Espasa Calpe.

IRWING, P. and LYNN, R. (2005), "Sex Differences in Means and Variability on the Progressive Matrices in University Students: a Meta-analysis", *British Journal of Psychology,* vol. 96(4): 505-524.

JONSSON, P. and CARLSSON, I. (2000), "Androgyny and Creativity: A Study of the Relationship between a Balanced Sex-Role and Creative Functioning", *Scandinavian Journal of Psychology,* vol. 41 (1): 269-274.

MOEBIUS, P. J. (1900), On the Mental Inferiority of Women, Leipzig.

STERNBERG, R. J. (1988), *The Triarchic Mind,* London, Penguin Books.

Chapter 7

BANDURA, A. (1977), "Self-Efficacy: Toward a Unifying Theory of Behavioral Change", *Psychological Review,* vol. 84(2): 191-215.

HACKETT, G. and BETZ, N. E. (1995), "Self-efficacy and Career Choice and Development", in MADDUX, J. E. (ed.), *Self-efficacy, Adaptation and Adjustment: Theory, Research and Application,* New York, Plenum.

MICHELLE R. CLAYMAN INSTITUTE FOR GENDER RESEARCH (2008), https://anitaborg.org/wp-content/uploads/2013/12/Climbing_the_Technical_Ladder.pdf, access 6 September 2016

SCHOLZ, U.; GUTIÉRREZ-DONA, B.; SUD, S. and SCHWARZER, R. (2002), "Is Perceived Self-efficacy a Universal Construct? Psychometric Findings from 25 Countries", *European Journal of Psychological Assessment,* vol. 18: 242-251.

WIGFIELD, A.; ECCLES, J. S. and PINTRICH, P. R. (1996), "Development Between the Ages of 11 and 25", in BERLINER, D. C. and CALFEE, R. C. (eds.), *Handbook of Educational Psychology,* New York, Simon & Schuster/Macmillan.

Chapter 8

AMERICAN PSYCHIATRIC ASSOCIATION (1994), *Diagnostic and Statistical Manual of Mental Disorders,* Washington D. C.

CARVER, C. S.; SCHEIER, M. F. and SEGERSTROM, S. C. (2010), "Optimism", *Clinical Psychology Review,* vol.30: 879-889.

HELGESON, V. S. and FRITZ, H. L. (1999), "Cognitive Adaptation as a Predictor of New Coronary Events Following Percutaneous Transluminal Coronary Angioplasty", *Psychosomatic Medicine,* vol. 61: 488-495.

KUBZANSKY, L. D.; SPARROW, D.; VOKONAS, P. and KAWACHI, I. (2001), "Is the Glass Half Empty or Half Full? A Prospective

Study of Optimism and Coronary Heart Disease in the Normative Aging Study", *Psychosomatic Medicine,* vol. 63: 910-916.

ROSENBERG, M. (1965), *Society and the Adolescent Self-Image,* New Jersey, Princeton.

SCHEIER, M. F. and CARVER, C. S. (1985), "Optimism, Coping and Health: Assessment and Implications of Generalized Outcome Expectancies", *Health Psychology,* vol. 4: 219-247.

SCHEIER, M. F.; CARVER, C. S. and BRIDGES, M. W. (1994), "Distinguishing Optimism from Neuroticism (and Trait Anxiety, Self-Mastery, and Self-Esteem), A Reevaluation of the Life Orientation Test", *Journal of Personality and Social Psychology,* vol. 67: 1063-1078.

ZAMBRANO, M. (1945), "Eloisa o la Esencia de la Mujer", *Revista Sur,* no. 124, Buenos Aires, from LAURENZI, E. and ZAMBRANO, M. (2004), *Nacer por sí misma,* Madrid, Horas y Horas-Cuadernos Inacabados.

Chapter 9

CAJAL, S. R. (1913), *Estudios sobre la degeneración y regeneración del sistema nervioso,* Madrid, Moya.

DÖBRÖSSY, M. D.; DRAPEAU, E.; AUROUSSEAU, C.; LE MOAL, M.; PIAZZA, P. V. and ABROUS, D. N. (2003), "Cell Death Promotes Learning Growth", *Molecular Psychiatry,* vol. 8 (12): 974-982. DWECK, C.

S. y REPPUCCI, D. N. (1973), "Learnt Helplessness and Reinforcement Responsibility in Children", *Journal of Personality and Social Psychology,* vol. 25: 109-116. FRANKL, V. E. (1979), *El hombre en busca de sentido,* Barcelona, Herder (original edition, 1946).

GILAD, B. (1982), "On Encouraging Entrepreneurship: An Interdisciplinary Approach", *Journal of Behavioral Economics,* vol. 11: 132-163.

GOULD, E.; REEVES, A.J.; GRAZIANO, M. S. and GROSS, C. G. (1999), "Neurogenesis in the Neocortex of Adult Primates", *Science,* vol. 286, no. 5439: 548-552.

KANT, I. (1981), Critique of Practical Reason, Madrid, Espasa Calpe (original edition,1788).

KAST, F.E. and ROSENZWEIG, J.E. (1979): Organisation and Management: A Systems and Contingency Approach (3rd edn.) (NewYork, McGraw Hill).

KENNEDY, P. (1989), *Auge y caída de las grandes potencias,* Barcelona, Plaza y Janés.

LOCKE, E. A. (1968), "Toward a Theory of Task Motivation and Incentives", *Organizational Behaviour and Human Performance,* vol. 3 (2): 157-189.

MAGAVI, S. S.; LEAVITT, B. R. and MACKLIS, J. D. (2000), "Induction of Neurogenesis in the Neocortex of Adult Mice", *Nature,* no. 405: 951-955.

ROTTER, J.B. (1966), "Generalized Expectancies for Internal Versus External Control of Reinforcement", *Psychological Monographs,* vol. 80 (1): 1-28.

SINKULA, J.M.; BAKER, W.E. and NOORDEWIER, T. (1997), "A Framework for Market-Based Organisational Learning: Linking Values, Knowledge, and Behaviour", *Journal of the Academy of Marketing Science,* vol. 25(4): 305-318.

VANDEWALLE, D. (2001), "Why Wanting to Look Successful Doesn't Always Lead to Success", *Organizational Dynamics,* vol. 30(2): 162-171.

Chapter 10

LEWIN, K. (1935) A dynamic theory of personality. New York: McGraw-Hill ·

LOCKE, E. A. (1968), "Toward a Theory of Task Motivation and Incentives", Organizational Behaviour and Human Performance, vol. 3(2): 157-189.

MASLOW, A. H. (1943), "A Theory of Human Motivation", *Psychological Review,* vol. 50(4): 370-396.

MCCLELLAND, D. C. (1961), *The Achievement Society,* New York, The Free Press.

MCGREGOR, D. (1960), *The Human Side of Enterprise,* New York, McGraw-Hill.

SKINNER, B. F. (1974), *About Behaviourism,* London, Jonathan Cape.

SMITH, R.; JAYASURIYA, R.; CAPUTI, P. and HAMMER, D. (2008), "Exploring the Role of Goal Theory in Understanding Training Motivation", *International Journal of Training and Development,* vol. 12 (1): 54-72.

THORNDIKE, E. L. (1911), *Animal Intelligence,* New York, Macmillan.

VROOM, V. H. (1964), *Work and Motivation,* New York, Wiley.

Chapter 11

DARWIN, C. (1998), The Expression of the Emotions in Man and Animals, New York, Oxford University Press (original edition, 1872).

DELEMEAU, J. (1978): La peur en Occident, Paris, Arthème Fayard.

HASSAN, M. K.; ENAYATULLAH and KHALIQUE, A. (1977), "A Study of Anxiety in School Children as Related to Child Rearing Attitudes and Some Personality Traits of Parents", Indian Journal of Psychiatric Social Work, vol. 6 (1): 1-7.

LAVACH, J. F. and LANIER, H. B. (1975), "The Motive to Avoid Success in.7th, 8th, 9th, and 10th Grade High-achieving Girls", The Journal of Educational Research, vol. 68 (6): 216-218.

SMITH, C. P. (1969), Achievement-related Motives in Children, New York, Russell Sage Foundation.

Chapter 14

EUROPEAN COMMISSION (2013), Women active in the ICT sector, Bruselas.

HEWLETT, S.A.; LUCE, C.B.; SERVON, L.J.; SHERBIN, L.; SHILLER, P.; SOSNOVICH, E. y SUMBERG, K. (2008), «The Athena Factor: Reversing the Brain Drain in Science, Engineering and Technology», Harvard Business Review, Boston.

MCKINSEY GLOBAL INSTITUTE (2011), Internet Matters: The Net's sweeping impact on growth, jobs, and prosperity (online): http:// www. mckinsey.com/insights/high_tech_telecoms_internet/internet_ matters, Access 6 September 2016

MCKINSEY GLOBAL INSTITUTE (2011), Big Data: The next frontier for innovation, competition and productivity (online): http://www.mckinsey. com/insights/business_technology/big_data_the_next_frontier_ for_innovation, access 2 January 2016